Presented to:

_____

From:

_____

SANCTUARY

FINDING MOMENTS
of REFUGE
in the PRESENCE OF GOD

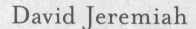

David Jeremiah

A Division of Thomas Nelson Publishers
Since 1798

Published in Nashville, Tennessee, by Thomas Nelson. Thomas Nelson is a
registered trademark of Thomas Nelson, Inc.

Published in association with Yates & Yates, LLP, Literary Agents, Orange,
California.

Thomas Nelson, Inc., titles may be purchased in bulk for educational,
business, fund-raising, or sales promotional use. For information, please
e-mail SpecialMarkets@ThomasNelson.com.

Unless otherwise indicated, Scripture quotations used in this book are from
THE NEW KING JAMES VERSION, © 1979, 1980, 1982, Thomas Nelson,
Inc. Used by permission. All rights reserved.

Other Scripture quotations are from the following sources:

HOLY BIBLE, NEW INTERNATIONAL VERSION (NIV), © 1973, 1978,
1984, International Bible Society. Used by permission of Zondervan Bible
Publishers.

NEW AMERICAN STANDARD BIBLE (NASB), © 1960, 1962, 1963, 1968,
1971, 1972, 1973, 1975, 1977, 1995 by the Lockman Foundation. Used by
permission.

The KING JAMES VERSION of the Bible (KJV).

The Living Bible (TLB), © 1971. Used by permission of Tyndale House Publishers,
Inc. Wheaton, Illinois 60189. All rights reserved.

ISBN 978-1-4003-1827-8

Printed in China

14 TIMS 5

TO MY LORD JESUS . . .
HE IS MY SANCTUARY AND
PLACE OF REFUGE

INTRODUCTION

You are awesome, O God, in your sanctuary; the God of Israel gives power and strength to His people. Praise be to God!

PSALM 68:35 NIV

Finding refuge is not a concept most of us relate to in the physical sense. We have our comfortable homes and vehicles and the freedom to come and go without restraint. The physical freedom we experience can sometimes hide the emotional need for refuge, until someone or something brings it all to the surface and we can't ignore the reality of our need. It is at this very point in time that our concept of God comes clearly into focus.

If we're not careful we can spend all our lives around the circumference of the circle of knowing God and never actually get to the center of it. It's easy to get caught up in the mechanics of living a Christian *lifestyle* and not truly understand what it means to live a Christian *life*.

Webster defines *sanctuary* as "sacred, a holy place, as a building set aside for worship, a place of refuge or protection." In the New Testament we are told that our bodies are the temples of God. We are to live as a sanctuary of His presence.

Many Christians make the mistake of thinking that just because they are believers in Christ, just because they read the Bible, just because they have the Holy Spirit living in them, they should be immune from the trials and pressures of this earthly life. Doctors' and counselors' offices are filled with sincere Christians who find it difficult, if not impossible, to maintain peace and perspective in a stress-filled world.

Oftentimes for Christians our practice comes first, and our theology follows behind it. We decide what we're going to do, and then we try to find a theology that makes us comfortable in doing it. But God is not affected by what we believe about Him. Our opinions of Him don't change who He is. If we don't know who He is, we may end up creating a God in our minds who meets our fancies or letting other people create God for us. We need to find God in His Word and through His Son, Jesus Christ. We need to know the God who is our refuge.

When Jesus was ready to go back to heaven, He gave one assignment to the apostles. He said, "Go therefore and make disciples of all the nations, baptizing them in the name of the Father and of the Son and of the Holy Spirit" (Matthew 28:19). Making disciples is one thing, but being a disciple is quite another without the next words He spoke: "Lo, I am with you always, even to the end of the age" (v. 20). God is with us! We celebrate that truth when we call Him "Immanuel." It means "God with us." Not God somewhere beyond the stars, but God *here with us*, encouraging us, ministering to us, helping us.

In times when we're tempted, we understand that He is here, and it brings us up short in our conduct. And in times when we have difficulties in life, we know that we don't go through them by ourselves. His consistent message through the whole Bible is that He will be *with us*. Because God is with us, we are His *sanctuary* and He is our Refuge.

JANUARY

≋

Do you not know that your body is the temple of the Holy
Spirit who is in you, whom you have from God?

—1 CORINTHIANS 6:19

THE AWESOME FACE OF GOD

*Give unto the LORD the glory due His name; worship the LORD
in the beauty of holiness.*

PSALM 29:2

As you meet with God in the light of morning, as your thoughts turn to Him in the adrenaline rush of the day, as you move into the silent sanctuary on the Lord's Day, know that He takes His place upon the throne whenever you give Him your praise. Your bowed head, your humbled heart, and your attentive spirit open the door to heaven. It's a door that swings both ways, for God comes to us no matter where we are.

The wonder of worship is the wonder of His very real presence. It's music from another world, wonder that floods out all the darkness and the dust of death this life contains. We rediscover the innocence of children again as we praise and exalt God's name, for He opens Himself to us. It's the most awesome moment of life—more awesome than holding your first child in the delivery room, more awesome than meeting the person you're destined to marry, more awesome than seeing the earth from the window of the space shuttle. You've seen something more beautiful: the face of God Himself.

David Jeremiah

LONG-DISTANCE FATHER

The eyes of the Lord are on the righteous, and His ears are open to their prayers.

1 PETER 3:12

When you became a son—when you were adopted into His family as a son or daughter of God—He opened up for you, through Christ's death on the cross, a way of fellowship and relationship that makes it possible for you to go right into His presence.

Do you relate to God like that? Are you in fellowship with Him? The way God "fathers" us will change the way we father our own children. Now that my children are grown and out of the house, I've had to apply God's principles of being available in new ways: I'm learning to be a "long-distance" father. I have entered into a deeper "relationship" with my internet server so as to fulfill my fathering responsibilities. Fathering from a distance has added some new expenses, but it is what I need to do to remain a father to my children.

Now, if I am like that as an earthly father with limited resources, how available do you think your spiritual Father in heaven is? You don't need a long-distance calling card or an 800 number. He is waiting for you to come into His presence in prayer at any time.

TRUST THE CHARACTER OF GOD

You are my hope, O Lord GOD; You are my trust from my youth.

PSALM 71:5

Sometimes during trials we focus so intently on our experience that we forget to focus on God. But the psalmist didn't. Over and over in this psalm he calls to mind the character and attributes of God: His glory, His power and strength, and His faithfulness.

And five times he mentions God's righteousness. The one thing that we must never lose sight of in the midst of our own suffering is the righteousness and goodness of God. It is because of God's inherent goodness that we are able to trust Him in all things.

When you are in the middle of trials, everyone will have an opinion or a suggestion or a remedy—and if they are from people you trust, you should consider them. But after all is said and done, there is only one thing that you can put all your trust in, and that is the character of God.

David Jeremiah

FILLED WITH THE ENCOURAGER

When [Barnabas] came and had seen the grace of God, he was glad, and
encouraged them all that with purpose of heart they should continue with the Lord.

ACTS 11:23

The Holy Spirit is the Encourager. Anyone who wants to be an encourager of others must be filled with the Encourager as Barnabas was. Because of the Spirit's presence in him, he could readily yield to the leading of God. Our own ego and drive for self-promotion is so strong that only the Spirit can bring about the transformation needed to accomplish God's purposes. When we build up and encourage others, we know that God is at work in and through us.

The fact that Barnabas was good, generous, gracious, and godly was not because of his upbringing or his education or his heritage. It was because he was filled with the Holy Spirit. The same Holy Spirit who indwelt Barnabas is the Spirit who is given to every believer in Jesus Christ. We receive the Holy Spirit when we are born again, and we remain filled with the Holy Spirit as we confess our sins and yield to His leading in our lives. God wants every Christian to be filled with the Encourager so that we might become encouragers as Barnabas was. The same glory brought to God through Barnabas's life can be brought to Him through our lives.

LOVE'S POWER

[Love] bears all things, believes all things, hopes all things, endures all things.

1 CORINTHIANS 13:7

Love hopes all things. Love that hopes has a confident expectation. It is a definite, persistent, absolute truth. There is no situation that divine love within us cannot face with full hope. That's what love is all about. Love hopes.

Hope is not refusing to face the truth. Hope is having a confidence in God to see you through each difficult trial. Jesus was always the epitome of truth, but He never failed to bring hope to others. When He met the woman taken in adultery, He inspired her to hope again. When He met the thief on the cross, Jesus made sure that man left this life with hope. He told the story about the lost coin that was found, and the lost son who came home, and the lost sheep that was found. Over and over again, what Jesus said in His messages was, "There's hope!" Though He was mocked, disbelieved, and crucified, He never doubted the glory that was yet to be, and He endured the cross for the joy that was set before Him. He had hope.

Love hangs on with tenacity when other hands let go in despair. To hope when faith has been disappointed is a greater thing than to have believed the sure thing. Love hopes all things.

David Jeremiah

LET'S SING!

Oh come, let us sing to the LORD! Let us shout joyfully to the Rock of our salvation.

PSALM 95:1

I sn't it wonderful that you could be on your hands and knees, scrubbing a filthy floor and singing the music of Zion?

Music helps you transport your spirit from mundane corners to majestic splendor. The body follows where the heart leads—and vice versa, as a matter of fact. Your prayers will be more focused and your mind more alert if you've aligned yourself on your knees. Some of your best worship might occur when you're jogging or driving a car, when your body is tensed to the task. Do you want to know how to incorporate worship into every moment of your day? Music is an excellent place to start.

Let's sing unto the Lord because it's one more way to give our bodies to His praises. Let's sing because music expresses levels of adoration we can't find in the spoken word. Let's sing because the people of the world will be attracted to our music. And let's sing because we absolutely can't help it! Our Lord reigns!

TEMPLE ON WHEELS

*I will dwell in [you] and walk [with you]. I will be [your] God
and [you] shall be My people.*

2 CORINTHIANS 6:16

We, the saints, were never meant to be restricted to one roof. What if you began to see yourself as a saint in circulation, a temple on wheels, so that God could say, "I will dwell in [you] and walk [with you]. I will be [your] God, and [you] shall be My people" (2 Corinthians 6:16). What if you took your worship on the road so that you rejoiced, prayed, expressed your thanksgiving, and exalted Him everywhere you went? You could think of yourself as a beautiful temple, a place fit for encasing the law of God, a place where all people could come to experience Him—for that's one essential element of a temple, isn't it? It's a place for others to come together in God's name. You may not have a ceiling and large rooms, but through you people can experience the living God just as they did in the old temple of Jerusalem. That's the very idea of having the Holy Spirit come to live within us. It isn't for the purpose of our having some private experience, but in order that we can serve God.

David Jeremiah

FAMILY OF GOD

Behold what manner of love the Father has bestowed on us,
that we should be called children of God!

1 JOHN 3:1

Perhaps you've been exposed to the idea of the "Fatherhood of God and the brotherhood of man." This idea suggests that God is the Father of us all, and we are all brothers regardless of who or where we are in life. In reality, there are two families in this world. There is the family of God, and there is the family of the devil. Until you are spiritually born again, you are not part of God's personal family—you cannot call Him "Father." There are many people who have gone all their lives without knowing God personally. They have prayed the Lord's Prayer, but to no avail, because you cannot pray "My Father" if He isn't really your Father. The way He becomes your Father is by your putting your trust in the gift He provided of His Son, Jesus Christ. When you accept Christ as Lord and Savior of your life, you become a child of God—you are born into His family, and He becomes your Father.

FROM SILENCE TO SINGING

You have turned for me my mourning into dancing; You have put off my sackcloth and clothed me with gladness, to the end that my glory may sing praise to You and not be silent.

PSALM 30:11–12

God is certainly with us when things are going well, but He is also with us when things aren't going so well. God is there when we achieve a major accomplishment or victory in life, but He is also there in the hospital room when we receive the bad news we were hoping not to hear. Whether in the ups or the downs, God is with us in every case.

The key thought is this: Whether you are going through weeping or joy, give thanks to God. Whether you are in an up time or a down time, give thanks to God. If you are experiencing prosperity or poverty, give thanks to God. If you are in times of dancing or of mourning, give thanks to God. Don't ever forget that the one constant in all of life is God's presence with you, and for that He deserves to be praised.

TAKE HIS HAND

I have come that they may have life, and that they may have it more abundantly.
JOHN 10:10

J esus Christ has proven that He has our absolute best interests at heart. What could He do that He has not done? He gave His life for us. Romans 5:8–10 says it this way:

> "But God demonstrates His own love toward us, in that while we were still sinners, Christ died for us. Much more then, having now been justified by His blood, we shall be saved from wrath through Him. For if when we were enemies we were reconciled to God through the death of His Son, much more, having been reconciled, we shall be saved by His life."

He is the one who said, "I have come that they may have life, and that they may have it more abundantly" (John 10:10). He gave His life for you, and if you will give Him your trust, not only will He give you today and forgive your sins, but He will give you the future. You can walk into that future with your hand in His, with a sense of confidence and with fear dispelled, knowing that He is your refuge and your strong tower.

HE IS THE LIGHT

The city had no need of the sun or of the moon to shine in it, for the glory of God illuminated it. The Lamb is its light.

REVELATION 21:23

Revelation 21:23 says plainly that there will be no sun or moon in heaven to provide illumination, because "the glory of God illuminated it. The Lamb is its light." We forget sometimes that there was light before God said, "Let there be light" (Genesis 1:3). God Himself is light "and in Him is no darkness at all" (1 John 1:5). Jesus said we are the light of the world (Matthew 5:14), but in reality we are only reflectors of His light. He is the only source of eternal light, for even our sun is slowly dying out. Light in heaven for eternity would have to come from the Light, which is God Himself.

No sun or moon means there will be no night. We will live constantly in the light in heaven. Think what that means for our lives: continual, uninterrupted fellowship and activity. The depression and discouragement that often accompany the darkness will be found nowhere in heaven.

David Jeremiah

FOLLOWING GOD'S SCHEDULE

I have glorified You on the earth. I have finished the work which You have given Me to do.

JOHN 17:4

Counselors often use a demonstration to help people see how they have compressed time with their frantic lifestyles. They will ask the client, on the "start" signal, to guess when they think a minute has passed. Most compulsive people and people suffering from addictions (even many normal people living in modern times) will say "stop" long before a minute has actually passed. For them, a minute is an eternity, and they drastically overestimate the speed of actual time. Why? Because their lives have become governed not by reality, but by unreality. It is unreal what people now try to accomplish in their lives. And because no one can live indefinitely at such a frantic pace, they turn to other things to sustain them.

Our perception of time must be geared to God's eternal perspective, not the perspective of the twenty-four hour day. The way Jesus lived His life is how we should live ours. Not in a hurry, not under insignificant deadlines, not burdened by unnecessary pressures. Rather, we should be moving in step with God's schedule. Following God's schedule, Jesus accomplished more in three years than anyone else could accomplish in a lifetime.

GOD'S PROVIDENCE

You gave me life and showed me kindness, and in your providence watched over my Spirit.

JOB 10:12 NIV

When Roger Williams arrived in the New World seeking religious liberty, he was opposed by some Puritans unfriendly to his views. Fleeing to Narragansett Bay, he purchased land and founded a settlement that later became the capital of Rhode Island. He named it Providence. It was a word, he felt, that aptly described God's ordering and over-ruling of his life.

We often find ourselves in difficult circumstances. But in both personal matters and global affairs, we can trust the overruling hand of our sovereign God, who turns negatives into positives, valleys into hills, and questions into exclamation marks. We can trust the providence of Him who has promised to work all things together for good.

Do you have a burden today? Worried about world events? Anxious about circumstances? A. W. Tozer wrote that the child of God travels in an appointed way. "Accidents may indeed appear to befall him," wrote Tozer, "but these evils will be so in appearance only and will seem evils only because we cannot read the secret script of God's providence."

David Jeremiah

FRIENDSHIP AND COMFORT

If you then, being evil, know how to give good gifts to your children, how much more will your Father who is in heaven give good things to those who ask him!

MATTHEW 7:11

Many people remain lonely because they fear rejection. They think rejection hurts worse than loneliness and spend much of their time and money trying to avoid it. But that is a wrong attitude. Those who expect to be rejected usually will feel that they are. Those who expect to receive friendship and comfort usually will.

When you need friendship and comfort, offer friendship and comfort, and don't expect rejection. Accept yourself where you are, whatever your need, and remember that Christ will not reject you. When you reach out to Him, He will always respond with loving acceptance. He says in Matthew 7:11, "If you then, being evil, know how to give good gifts to your children [and your friends and all those around you], how much more will your Father who is in heaven give good gifts to those who ask Him!"

Your greatest source of comfort and hope is Christ Jesus.

Our Immortality in Christ

So when this . . . mortal has put on immortality, then shall be brought to pass the saying that is written: "Death is swallowed up in victory."

1 Corinthians 15:54

People addicted to the need for recognition want their name to live forever. A famous real estate developer in our day has built and acquired numerous properties and buildings in New York City and attached his name to all of them. Perhaps he thinks that if he can get his name on enough things he will be immortal and that, after his death, his name will live on. The problem is that moth and rust eventually corrupt, and thieves break in and steal (Matthew 6:19). To what will the name be attached then?

If you know the Word of God, you know that immortality does not come from our achievements, but from a relationship with the Lord Jesus Christ. While it is true that every person will live forever, only those in Christ will truly live.

If you know the Lord, you don't have to worry about immortality. It's yours. God has given it to you as part of your gift of eternal life. You don't have to do all the things people do today to make sure they are remembered forever. If you live and die in Jesus Christ, you will be immortal.

David Jeremiah

CROWN OF CREATION

What is man that You are mindful of him, and the son of man that You visit him? For You have made him a little lower than the angels, and You have crowned him with glory and honor.

PSALM 8:4–5

The night sky casts a divine, pensive spell over us, as people have found through the ages; God designed it to do so. David the psalmist, who gazed out upon those stars during so many nights of watching over his sheep, must have continually marveled. And he must have realized who was watching over him. As he considered his Lord, according to the psalm, he finally was brought to consider himself. "Who am I that I would be worthy of even a thin moment of Your attention?" he wondered. "I look upon the crown of Your creation, and I wonder: how is it that You could place a crown upon me?" For David, of course, a royal destiny did beckon. But true worship has this effect upon us: it simultaneously humbles and uplifts us. In other words, worship places us exactly where we should be, in the realization that we are small, yet a little lower than the angels; we are tiny creatures in the presence of God, but tiny creatures whom He adores.

CALL UPON GOD

The LORD gives wisdom; from His mouth come knowledge and understanding.

PROVERBS 2:6

The prerequisite to obtaining help in dealing with our troubles is to realize that we lack sufficient wisdom to sort them out! The argument is this: "When facing trials, it is important to know how to cope with them. The only way we will be able to understand these trials and respond to them properly is by asking for the wisdom that only God can give." When our friends and loved ones are going through trials, we may think we see what God is doing through the ordeal. But when we are the sufferers, when we are the ones going through the fire, viewing the situation from God's perspective is a little more difficult. For this reason we are to ask God for wisdom.

As James motivates the troubled believer to seek wisdom (James 1:5), he describes God in such a way as to make us wonder why we have waited so long to reach out for His help.

We know from the Scriptures that God is the source of true wisdom. He is a good God who is not partial to any. He will always answer the prayer for wisdom, never turning away such a request. He may not always answer on our time schedule, but He always answers.

RECEIVED INTO HIS PRESENCE

He who did not spare His own Son, but delivered Him up for us all,
how shall He not with Him freely give us all things?

ROMANS 8:32

If there was ever a person who had room to complain of injustice, it was Jesus. He was the only innocent man to be punished by God. If we stagger at the wrath of God, let us stagger at the cross. The cross was at once the most horrible and the most beautiful example of the wrath of God. God loves us with an everlasting love and wants to bring us to be with Him forever. But God is absolutely holy, and in order for us to be with Him, He had to deal with the issue of holiness. So He sent His holy Son and let Him suffer the penalty of sin for everyone. And then He gave those who trusted in His Son the full benefits of righteousness. He gave us the holiness of His Son.

When we stand before God in His holiness, He looks at us and sees the righteous clothing of His flawless Son. He is able to receive us into His presence. God is so holy that He would not even spare His own Son in order that we might have fellowship with Him.

PUTTING IT INTO WORDS

I cry out to the LORD with my voice; with my voice to the LORD I make my supplication.

PSALM 142:1

When we verbalize our feelings and concerns to God, it is like entering into a conversation with an intimate friend. It is, in fact, a healthy way for us to open up and reveal what is inside, to bring up from the depths of our heart those things we may have stuffed down inside. Fortunately, God is not shocked or surprised by anything, so there is nothing we cannot tell Him. It is an insult to the One who tells us to cast all our cares upon Him not to do so (1 Peter 5:7).

Why would He tell us to verbalize our problems to Him if He did not mean for us to? Even psychologists tell us that verbalizing our problems, whether in writing or out loud, is a good way to bring clarity and definition to what are often very confusing feelings. Suddenly, as we put our feelings into words, we actually begin to see things more clearly ourselves—all because God is willing to listen.

David Jeremiah

GOD'S FAMILY

When Jesus therefore saw his mother, and the disciple whom he loved standing by, He said to his mother, "Woman, behold your son!" And he said to the disciple, "Behold your mother!"

JOHN 19:26–27

Our Lord emphasized the human family, but even more, He emphasized the spiritual family of God. The genuine and abiding relationship is not that of the flesh, but of the Spirit. As wonderful as earthly relationships are, there is a more intimate relationship between the children of God. John, as a believer, was a better choice to care for Jesus' mother than His brothers and sisters who did not believe.

Jesus brought into being the brotherhood of believers. He created a new society that is not segregated by race or nationality, nor predicated upon social standing or economic power. It consists of those whose faith meets at the cross and whose experience of forgiveness flows from it. Jesus commended His own mother into the hands of a brother. At Golgotha that terrible day, Christ called upon a brother in the family of faith to minister to someone in need. That is still part of His call to those in God's family.

THE MISSING PIECE IS CHRIST

In Him dwells all the fullness of the Godhead bodily; and you are complete in Him.

COLOSSIANS 2:9–10

Insight into who you are and why you are here is available only from the Creator, because you were created for Him. The missing piece in your life is not more education or better therapy. The missing piece in your life, if you don't know Christ, is to put Him at the center where He belongs. God created you uniquely for Himself. He put a vacuum within you that cannot be filled with anything else but Him. When you stuff in all the pleasure and all the madness of this age trying to find meaning in life, you will never discover it. But something happens when you say a simple prayer, giving in to God and receiving Him into your life.

Then Jesus comes to live within you. God loves you, He knows you, He has a plan for your life. He wants you to know who you are and why you are here, and if you will put your trust in Him, He will give you that perspective in your life. You were created in God's image, so you are really only yourself in relationship to God. When you let God take control of your life through His Son, life begins to have some meaning.

David Jeremiah

GOD IS THE CURE

He Himself has said, "I will never leave you nor forsake you."
HEBREWS 13:5

What is loneliness? I don't know how to define it; all I can do is describe it. It's an underlying anxiety at having no one close, a sharp ache in a moment of grief, and an empty feeling in the pit of the stomach when we know we have no one to whom we can turn. There is no anguish like loneliness.

But God has a cure for loneliness. In our walk with Him, He offers friendship, a family, and a peace that passes all understanding. When we meet Him, we are not guaranteed never to feel lonely, but we are promised that we will never be alone. After all, He is the one who said, "I will never leave you nor forsake you" (Hebrews 13:5).

PREPARE FOR TESTS

Of His own will He brought us forth by the word of truth, that we might be a kind of firstfruits of His creatures.

JAMES 1:18

James reminds us that we experience temptation because we are God's special people. We are members of His family because we have been born again by the word of truth. When James uses the word *firstfruits* to describe believers, he is reminding us that we belong only to God. In the Old Testament, firstfruits were the firstborn of cattle and the early fruit of the ground, both of which belonged to God.

The enemy targets us because of our relationship with God. There would be no inner battle if we were truly lost.

The tests God allows to mature us can become temptations from Satan that malign us. We must be prepared for tests, realize that they can become temptations, and then overcome them through the strength of our relationship with God.

David Jeremiah

WORSHIP AND WONDER

They were filled with wonder and amazement at what had happened to him.

ACTS 3:10

Worship and wonder, which are so closely connected, are all about coming to the end of our measurements. In the presence of Almighty God, as the apostle John discovered, the sense of wonder comes naturally and leaves us changed. How could we respond any other way? But without the capability of awe, where we stand at the edge of ourselves and gaze beyond, we will never come into His presence.

Do you ever wonder? How long has it been since you've been a child again, gaping with wide eyes? How would it change your life if you could live like that every day? How would it change the people around you?

I hope you're already sensing it—your heart's very desire. This is what has been lacking in so many lives. We've wandered through the emptiness when we could have been wondering at the fullness of the love of God. Your heart's desire, even if you haven't come to realize it, is to live every moment in the wonder of worship.

JOY IN THE MORNING

Weeping may endure for a night, but joy comes in the morning.

PSALM 30:5

I t's interesting that David follows a pattern of looking at the day that was begun in the creation account in Genesis. He says that weeping comes in the night, but joy comes in the morning. If you remember, when God created the heavens and the earth, He said, "The evening and the morning were the first day" (Genesis 1:5). We think just the opposite, don't we? We think of a day as the morning followed by the evening.

I think there are wonderful truths embedded in God's perspective on life. If you will look at your day as the evening and the morning instead of the morning and the evening, you will begin your day in the evening by meditating on what you need to accomplish the next day and asking God's blessing on it. Then He is free to work in your heart and mind as you sleep to prepare you for accomplishing those things. When Christ returns, there will be no more weeping. Weeping is ours during the night, but our eternal joy is coming in the morning of Christ's return.

A RESOURCE OF POWER

I tell you the truth: It is expedient for you that I go away; for if I go not away, the Comforter will not come unto you; but if I depart, I will send Him unto you.

JOHN 16:7 KJV

As a child of God, the Holy Spirit lives within my heart. Christ came into the world; He died; He was buried; He was resurrected; and He ascended into heaven. Before He ascended, He said, "Before I go, I want you to know I am going to send a Comforter who is not only going to be with you—He is going to be in you." The Holy Spirit is that Comforter whom Christ sent to live within us. By virtue of my sonship, I have a permanent spiritual resource—the Holy Spirit living within me. He helps me to walk, talk, and live like a son of God, something I couldn't do if He weren't within me. The standard for living life as a child of God is far beyond anything I could ever produce on my own. But when Christ came to live within my heart, He put His blessed Holy Spirit within me. Because I have the Spirit of the Father in me, I am identified as one of His children.

The Holy Spirit in me is far better than a calling card. With the Holy Spirit, I have access to my heavenly Father at any time. That is a resource of power that I cannot have any other way.

THE DESERVING ONE

The hour is coming, and now is, when the true worshipers will worship the
Father in spirit and truth; for the Father is seeking such to worship Him.

JOHN 4:23

When Lawrence of Arabia was in Paris with some of his Arab friends after World War I, he took them to see the sights of the city. His friends showed little interest in the Louvre, the Arch of Triumph, or Napoleon's tomb. The thing that really interested them was the faucet in their bathtub. They spent much time turning it on and off; they thought it was wonderful. All they had to do was turn the handle and they could get all the water they wanted.

When they were leaving Paris, Lawrence found them in the bathroom with wrenches, trying to get the faucet off so they could take it with them. "You see," they said, "it is very dry in Arabia. What we need are faucets. If we have them, we will have all the water we want." Lawrence had to explain to them that the effectiveness of the faucet depended on the water system to which it was attached.

Our study of worship reminds us that the effectiveness of all that we do in the church is not to be found in outward activity or service, but in the One who stands behind it. The One we serve. The One deserving of our worship.

CHANGE THROUGH CHRIST

Therefore, if anyone is in Christ, he is a new creation; old things have passed away; behold, all things have become new.

2 CORINTHIANS 5:17

I believe that for marriage to become the treasure the Bible says it can be, Jesus Christ must be at the center. When Jesus Christ comes into a life, that person gains the basic equipment necessary to become "one" with another person, to be secure in identity, someone who doesn't have to prove personal worth because he or she recognizes that worth in Jesus Christ. The best thing that can happen to any marriage is for both partners to know Jesus Christ as their personal Savior and walk with Him by faith.

Would you like to know a priceless secret? Here it is: God is awesome and He'll change your life, He'll change your marriage, He'll change your family, and He'll change your future for generations to come. That's what God, through Christ, will do!

He is waiting for you to give Him an invitation into your life. He does not barge in where He is not wanted. If you will take the initiative today, you can begin right now to live as you were meant to live. When you do, you will start to personally experience the awesomeness of God at work in your marriage and family. And when that happens, anything is possible.

JESUS IS THE LIFE

Jesus said to her, "I am the resurrection and the life. He who believes in Me, though he may die, he shall live. And whoever lives and believes in Me shall never die."

JOHN 11:25–26

The King of kings came into the world humbly. He was born in a stable, His cradle a feed trough. In His thirty-three years of earthly life, He owned no possessions. He had to depend on others to provide for His needs, and He had to borrow everything He used. The stable where He was born was borrowed. He borrowed money to pay His taxes, a boat to stand in and preach, a cross on which to die. Even His tomb was not His own.

But He had a mission that He alone could accomplish: He, the Son of Man, came "to seek and to save that which was lost" (Luke 19:10). He bore our sins "in His own body on the tree" that in the age to come we might have eternal life (1 Peter 2:24; Mark 10:29–30; and John 3:13–17). Of Himself He says, "I am the resurrection and the life. He who believes in Me, though he may die, he shall live. And whoever lives and believes in Me shall never die" (John 11:25–26). He "put away sin by the sacrifice of Himself . . . so Christ was offered once to bear the sins of many . . . We have been sanctified through the offering of the body of Jesus Christ once for all" (Hebrews 9:26–10:10).

David Jeremiah

GOD ALWAYS KNEW YOU

For you formed my inward parts; You covered me in my mother's womb.
PSALM 139:13

God knew you before you were born. He knows the moment when you were conceived. In every phase of development, from that moment on, He is there. The human embryo is not the result of a biological accident. God is aware of the union of the sperm and the egg and the attachment of the embryo to the uterine lining and the development of human life. God formed the inward parts and arranged the genetic structure. God knows about that human life and loves that human life from the very moment of its union.

In every cell of your body there is enough information to re-create your adult person as if no other cell were necessary. And every time that cell divides in the process of your growth, all the information contained in each cell is part of the division. Someone has reasoned that if all of the instructions in the DNA of one cell were written out, it would take a thousand six-hundred-page books to put all that information down. And God put it in a cell that no one can see without magnification. And it's in every cell of your body. God did it so you would have your identity. You are unique. You are individually precious to God.

MAYBE NOT!

Lift up your eyes and look at the fields, for they are already white for harvest!
JOHN 4:35

Tenessee pastor Robert Shockey doesn't believe in chance encounters. To him, every contact is an opportunity to evangelize. When he answers the phone, for example, and hears the person on the other end saying, "Sorry, I must have the wrong number," Bob responds: "Maybe not!"

Usually there is a pause on the line, followed by something like, "What do you mean?" That gives Shockey an opening to initiate a conversation about the gospel. He has led more than one person to faith in Christ that way.

Evangelist Billy Graham once answered the phone in his hotel room. The person on the other end asked for so-and-so, and Mr. Graham told him he had the wrong number. There was a pause, and the person said, "You sure sound a lot like Billy Graham."

"This is Billy Graham," replied the evangelist. During the ensuing conversation, the caller gave his life to Christ. There are opportunities all around us to witness for Christ, some in unexpected places. We are ambassadors for Christ—harvesters, witnesses. Perhaps the Holy Spirit will lead you to someone today who needs a word from the Lord.

FEBRUARY

≈

*In the world you will have tribulation, but be of good
cheer; I have overcome the world.*

—JOHN 16:33

REST IN JESUS

In the world you will have tribulation, but be of good cheer;
I have overcome the world.

JOHN 16:33

When we don't know how this is all going to work out, we have to hold tightly to the Lord Jesus Christ Himself and rest in Him. That's the message we often find in the New Testament.

In John 16:33, Jesus said to His disciples, "These things I have spoken to you, that in Me you may have peace. In the world you will have tribulation; but be of good cheer, I have overcome the world." Jesus had been talking about His future death, but then He said, "Don't get caught up in that. Make sure in the midst of these tumultuous times your trust is in Me."

When we go through a tough time, if we've spent any time at all in the Word of God, that tough time is like a magnet that draws us to the Lord Jesus. Nothing will happen in the future that will catch Jesus Christ by surprise. And there's nothing that will happen that He can't help His children work through.

So rather than spending our time trying to figure out the nuances of what will happen, we should spend at least as much time getting to know Him better.

David Jeremiah

THE POOR RICH MAN

For where your treasure is, there your heart will be also.

MATTHEW 6:21

A certain Muslim lived in a cottage on a hill. Every week he rode his camel to a little stream. And every week as the camel stopped to drink, it nosed up the pebbles in order to make a deeper place for drinking. Again and again, the Muslim picked up the bright stones the animal uncovered and took them home with him.

One day, a traveler told the Muslim of the easy comfort and riches that certain men in the city enjoyed; the traveler filled the Muslim's eyes and heart with discontent. So he sold his cottage and wandered the earth looking for money. Finally he died in rags and poverty, and was buried. The man who bought the cottage found the stones and preserved them.

One day, a merchant came to his home and discovered that these well-preserved stones were diamonds. The owner of the diamonds immediately became a millionaire. The first man had great wealth but, being ignorant of it, sold it and traveled the world looking for it. The second man simply made use of what he had. All people have eternal life at their disposal. Some respond to this treasure like the first man, some like the second.

COUNT IT ALL JOY

My brethren, count it all joy when you fall into various trials.

JAMES 1:2

Persecution was the most common trial among Jewish believers in James's time. Today, a trial can be a number of things: the loss of a job, a divorce, trouble with our children, severe financial strain, illness or death in the family, or relational problems over which we seem to have little control. Though our trials may not seem as severe as the persecution of James's day, note that James does not say "if" we encounter trials, but "when" we encounter trials. And when these trials come, our first strategy, according to James, is to "count it all joy."

To count, or consider, it all joy in the midst of our trials is to respond with a deliberate, intelligent appraisal of our situation. We must learn to look at our situation from God's perspective and recognize that, though the trial is not a happy experience in itself, it is God's way of producing something of great value. The word *count* means "to think in terms of the future." James is not saying we are to rejoice over pain, but we are to rejoice because God's purposes are being accomplished in our lives.

David Jeremiah

STAND AMAZED

God saw everything that He had made, and indeed it was very good.

GENESIS 1:31

Genesis begins, as everyone knows, with the creation of the world. None of us was there to witness it, but we're given the account of how God fashioned the heavens and the earth with His powerful hand. Through writing inspired by the Spirit of God, we can stand and behold the moment when God said, "Let there be light," when He divided the waters from the dry land, when He caused the earth to bring forth grass, and when He placed the sun, the moon, and the stars in the sky. On each occasion we know that God said, "It is good."

Yes, it is good! That's our most basic response, too, when we look into the star-filled sky or see the sun rise in glory over a mountain, bathing the skies in orange and deep blue. But when we see that which is perfect, that which God has proclaimed good, we respond also with our emotions. We stand amazed; we wonder. And that's a point we must stop and consider, for the ability to marvel lies at the very center of our identities as human beings created in the divine image.

Stand before that sunset. Not only will your eyes be filled, but also your very soul and imagination.

FROM WEEPING TO JOY

I will turn their mourning to joy, will comfort them, and make them rejoice rather than sorrow.

JEREMIAH 31:13

Sadness is an everyday truth in this life, and one we have to reckon with. But just as a day can bring sadness with it, it is also true that the day of sadness passes. We can be accused of being trite or trivial when we say it, but it is true that "things are going to get better; just hang on; you'll get through this." That's the truth. Sadness does turn to joy.

I don't know how many times I have faced a group of family and friends who have lost a loved one unexpectedly— a funeral can be the saddest day of our lives. Looking at people's faces, we wonder if they will ever smile again. And yet, I will see those same people in a matter of weeks or months and the joy has returned. It's just the process of life. We weep and then we rejoice. God gives us the grace to move from one phase to the next, from one day to the next.

David Jeremiah

YOUR WILL BE DONE

Your kingdom come, Your will be done on earth as it is in heaven.

MATTHEW 6:10

It is a helpless, hopeless feeling to be caught in a whirlpool in which other people and their priorities are sucking you under. I know that my priorities are God first, my wife next, my children next, and my vocation and ministry last. What a joy it is to go to God in prayer each day and pray what I have learned from the Lord's Prayer: "Lord, Your kingdom come, Your will be done. By the grace of God, with all that I have within me, Lord, help me this day to make Your will manifest in my life."

I have to keep praying that every day. I pray those priorities back to God, not only because I want God to hear them, but because I want *me* to hear them, so I don't ever forget. God changes us through prayer—when we pray, we get on the same wavelength with God. And as we pray, if we pray according to the will of God, little by little He takes all the things that are out of sync in our lives and puts them into sync so that we can take this big deep breath and say, "Oh, yes, that's the way it's supposed to be!"

PARENTING BY FAITH

Children, obey your parents in the Lord, for this is right. . . . And you, fathers, do not provoke your children to wrath, but bring them up in the training and admonition of the Lord.

EPHESIANS 6:1, 4

There is no such thing as painless parenting. Pain—even excruciating pain—is a natural part of the family process in our broken world. Women know better than anyone that pain is how the family got started. And the aches and pains, the hurts and hassles, will continue to intrude into the parenting pathway through the years, whether we like it or not.

That's why a vital faith in Jesus Christ is so crucial to a happy family. God equips us through faith to meet all the challenges of parenting, even in a toxic environment. Consider Ephesians 6:1, for example: "Children, obey your parents." How? "In the Lord." Or read Ephesians 5:25: "Husbands, love your wives." How? "As Christ loved the church." Or Ephesians 5:22: "Wives, submit to your own husbands." How? "As to the Lord." All these instructions to the family wrap around a core of faith in God and Jesus Christ.

Don't try to build your family without faith in God. Throw yourself on His grace and mercy and say to Him, "Lord, I know that apart from You, I can't do anything but mess this thing up. So I'm going to hang on to You with both hands. Together, we'll make this family work."

David Jeremiah

GOD IS GRACIOUS

If any of you lacks wisdom, let him ask of God, who gives to all liberally and without reproach, and it will be given to him.

JAMES 1:5

James says that God gives to all men "liberally," which means two things. First, the word means "to stretch out," and it pictures God stretching or spreading out His table of wisdom. God dispenses His wisdom to those of us who ask by lavishly pouring out to us the full supply of that which we need. The second meaning reflects the word *singly*. God is the opposite of the "double-minded" man mentioned in 1:8. God gives His wisdom simply, plainly, and individually to all who will ask of Him.

God also gives His wisdom without reproach (that is, without insult). When we pray for wisdom, God does not scold us for coming. He is a God who is generous and gracious, so seekers should approach Him in faith. If we approach God without faith, we have decided to live life our own way, to make our own decisions, to separate ourselves from Him.

James says the person who prays while doubting is like a wave of the sea, blown and tossed about by the wind. However, the faithful man is stable, looking in only one direction for the wisdom he needs. And he knows that the God to whom he prays is able and willing to respond to his need.

CHRIST CURES

[Christ] Himself bore our sins in His own body on the tree, that we, having died to sins, might live for righteousness—by whose stripes you were healed.

1 PETER 2:24

For true comfort we must turn to the Master Healer. The apostle Peter gives us the promise of healing when we turn to Christ, "Who Himself bore our sins in His own body on the tree, that we, having died to sins, might live for righteousness—by whose stripes you were healed. For you were like sheep going astray, but have now returned to the Shepherd and Overseer of your souls" (1 Peter 2:24–25).

We are comforted by the knowledge that because of our Savior's lonely suffering and death and His glorious resurrection, we also will rise again to have eternal life in heaven. Even when our loved ones die and leave us behind, we can become true survivors in Christ and not be overwhelmed by the pain of separation and aloneness, for we are not forever separated from them nor are we ever truly alone. Our Savior is always with us, and through His power we know that the death of an earthly body is not the end of life, but the beginning of eternal happiness. Knowing this gives us comfort.

David Jeremiah

WALK BY FAITH

For we walk by faith, not by sight.

2 CORINTHIANS 5:7

Faith is seeking and finding God in Christ—desiring Him and being fulfilled by Him. To say it another way, faith is wholly leaning on Christ for everything in your life. It is trusting Him for eternity. Faith is the acceptance of a gift at the hand of Almighty God. That's what faith is, and anything that doesn't meet that standard, while it may be a spiritual term, is not faith. The Bible tells us that not only do we walk by faith and live by faith every day, but faith also plays a part in our life as we continue to seek a deeper relationship with God through Jesus Christ.

We have a problem in that we have isolated faith to the act of becoming a Christian instead of living the ongoing Christian life. Certainly, faith is at the center of our entrance into salvation. But if we leave it there and do not continue to exercise faith daily, we will fail to live an obedient spiritual life. We literally must walk by faith as believers or we will not walk at all.

NO QUALITY WITHOUT QUANTITY

You shall teach [God's commands] diligently to your children, and shall talk of them when you sit in your house, when you walk by the way, when you lie down, and when you rise up.

DEUTERONOMY 6:7

It's not the quantity but the quality of time that really counts. Simply defined, the statement means that one can make up for having minimal moments with his family by making certain that the time he does have is quality time.

On the surface, this concept seems to make a lot of sense. It is possible to spend much time with one's family that is seemingly meaningless. All of us experience times when we are at home physically but our minds are wandering miles away. I can remember days with the family that could have been "scratched" in terms of quality.

So what is the "quality time" myth? It's as phony as the fake diamond in a one-dollar ring. The fact is, there is no quality without quantity. Too many parents live with the regrets of abandoned moments. It takes time to be silly, to share a secret, to heal a hurt, to kiss away a tear. Moments of uninhibited communication between child and parent cannot be planned; they just happen. The only ingredient we bring to that dynamic of family life is our availability . . . and that is spelled T-I-M-E.

David Jeremiah

FINDING REAL LOVE

But the fruit of the Spirit is love.

GALATIANS 5:22

I'm convinced that what we need most in our world today—in our churches, in our homes, and in our personal lives—is a great outpouring of *agape* love. It is not an accident that God has put love at the top of the list of the fruit of the Spirit, because when that is right, everything else has the greatest potential to fall into place.

How can we get this love in our lives? By finding out how much God really loves us. We love Him because He first loved us.

If your heart is filled with bitterness, resentment, and hard feelings, God loves you just as you are in spite of that. But when you go to His Word and contemplate His love for you, when you see the price He paid that you might have Him and His love, when you drink deeply of His love and thank Him for loving you, the wonder of it all begins to break in on your consciousness.

Then real love, *agape* love, God's love, can begin to develop in your life. Get caught up in how God loves you, and watch your life respond. The more we know about God and His love for us, the more that love begins to fill our being until we become like Him.

THE BEST LOVE

Let each of you look out not only for his own interests,
but also for the interests of others.

PHILIPPIANS 2:4

There is an inscription on a small tombstone in an English village that reads: "Here lies a miser who lived for himself. He cared for nothing but gathering wealth. Now, where he is or how he fares, nobody knows and nobody cares."

The root of all evil in human nature is the desire to have one's own say. Self-centeredness is the exact opposite of *agape* love. *Agape* love is love that seeks the best interest of the one loved. Selfishness seeks the best interest for one's own self, so the two are exactly opposite. It is not possible to have *agape* love and to have self-seeking or self-interest. R. C. H. Lenski, the well-known commentator, has said, "If you can cure selfishness, you have just replanted the Garden of Eden." It was selfishness that caused Adam and Eve to reject God's way in favor of their own desires. Self replaced God in their hearts, and they determined to go their own way. Love, on the other hand, is not interested in its own way but is preoccupied with the interests of others.

Love does not seek its own. Love considers the other person and gets excited about seeing that their needs get met.

David Jeremiah

ONLY LOVE

If God so loved us, we also ought to love one another.

1 JOHN 4:11

A famous psychiatrist once said, "Love, true love, is the medicine for our sick old world. If people can learn to give and receive love, they will usually recover from their physical and mental illnesses."

Before Christ, the concept of love was a love for the best. If something was deemed worthy of love, it was loved. Christ dying on the cross changed all that, for He offered a love for which we are completely unworthy. Christ revealed God's love. He lavished that holy love on people with no thought about whether they were worthy or not. Now when a Christian wants to know what real love is, he looks to the cross. Having experienced God's love while yet a sinner, and having been transformed by that great love, the Christian recognizes the people around him as the objects of God's love. They are love-starved, in need of the transforming power that only Christ's love can bring.

Jesus set an example by giving Himself totally in love, with no thought of receiving anything in return. We, as Christians, are called by God to reflect that love to our spouses, our families, and our world. And the more we reflect it, the more we give it away to others, the more we experience it in our own lives.

LISTEN TO JESUS

I am the First and the Last. I am He who lives, and was dead, and behold, I am alive forevermore.

REVELATION 1:17–18

Who is Jesus? He's the Son of God and the Son of man. He is the God-man and the man-God. He is Jesus Christ, the Son of the Living God. He is God walking around in a body. He is God forever enthroned in heaven, now at the right hand of the Father. Jesus Christ is God.

One of the greatest illustrations of who Christ is and why we should listen to His words is found in the prologue of the book of Revelation. John was in exile on the isle of Patmos, and he saw this One to whom we are appealing and said, "When I saw Him, I fell at His feet as dead. But He laid His right hand on me, saying to me, 'Do not be afraid; I am the First and the Last. I am He who lives, and was dead, and behold, I am alive forevermore. Amen'" (1:17–18).

There is no one like Jesus Christ. He is the only one who has ever lived or ever will live who has a true grasp of the future. Because the Lord Jesus Christ as God lives in the time about which He speaks, He views all of time as if it were the present. He is the Eternal One, the Alpha and the Omega, the Beginning and the End, the First and the Last.

David Jeremiah

THE PERIL OF RELIGION

The Pharisee stood and prayed thus with himself, "God, I thank you that I am not like other men—extorters, unjust, adulterers, or even as this tax collector."
LUKE 18:11

One of the terrible possibilities suggested by the Pharisee's attitude in prayer is this: a person can be religious and not be right. This man's religion became the cause of his ruin. He did everything right from a religious perspective— in fact, more than right! His problem was that he had totally excluded God from the picture of his life. His religion was all about him.

Every Sunday, people attend houses of worship with other worshipers. They sing hymns, recite liturgies, pray prayers, listen to sermons. And they will leave feeling better about themselves than when they went in. Unfortunately, they will still be deeply rooted in their sins. If our religion does nothing more than make us feel better about our sin, then that religion has doomed us, not saved us.

The Pharisee was a religious man who was lost in his religion. Along with everything else we learn in this story, we learn about the dangers of religious pride. And that doesn't mean we are to go to a church where we leave feeling bad. It means we are to leave feeling good about the Savior whose mercy has saved us from our sins. We leave feeling good about God's justification, not our own.

ALONE WITH GOD

In the morning my prayer comes before you.

PSALM 88:13

I believe the best time to get alone with God is early morning—it sets the tone for your entire day. He'll show you things and tell you things that will make the difference at crisis points during the next twelve hours or so. After you talk with the Lord and walk with Him through the schedule that lies ahead of you, He'll strengthen and encourage you to make every point of your day an act of worship.

Another advantage to a morning time with God is that He'll plant His Word in your heart. You'll be amazed at how often the very verse you studied over your morning coffee will have key significance a few hours later. Ask the Spirit to illuminate your study, and then go over your Scripture passage reflectively. Try to take that verse with you the rest of the day so that it's never far from your mind. The Word of God is essential to the worship of God, and there's simply nothing so encouraging as His timeless and powerful Word. One little verse is enough to give you a divine perspective throughout the day.

David Jeremiah

GOD'S ALWAYS THERE

When my spirit was overwhelmed within me, then You knew my path.

PSALM 142:3

A friend of mine likes to tell about the time his grand-daughter told him what she learned in Sunday school: that God never says, "Oops!"

There is profound theological truth in that little girl's remembrance of her lesson. God didn't look down from heaven surprised to find David in a cave in a fit of discouragement—and David knows it. He says to God, "When my spirit was overwhelmed within me, then You knew my path." God knew right where David was the whole time—all the time David was discouraged, deserted, depressed, and defeated. God was there the whole way.

For some reason, we are greatly tempted to think that because no one else is around, God isn't either; because no one else knows how we feel, God doesn't either; because no one else is willing to listen, God isn't either. God is always there, and to recognize that is the first step toward meeting His solutions to our dilemma.

ONE DAY AT A TIME

Give us this day our daily bread.

MATTHEW 6:11

Every day I try to pray, "God, I want Your will to be done on earth as it is in heaven. Please meet my needs today." To trust Him daily presupposes that you talk to Him daily. Praying week to week is not in the Lord's Prayer. The challenges of life come daily, not weekly. For us to remain free of worry, we have to pray and trust Him daily.

It's not wrong to think about tomorrow, to plan for tomorrow, or to make provision for tomorrow. It's just wrong to worry about tomorrow. I believe God expects me to plan as if it all depends on me but pray as if it all depends on Him.

The only way we get through crises with our kids is one day at a time. The only way we get through sickness is one day at a time. The only way we get through times of financial stress is one day at a time. Why? Because God has ordained that life moves at the pace of one day at a time. All He wants us to do is be in step with Him—to trust Him for today.

David Jeremiah

THE ENERGY TO WAIT

*He did not waver at the promise of God through unbelief . . . being fully
convinced that what He had promised He was also able to perform.*

ROMANS 4:20–21

One of the hardest things for us to do is wait on God. Sometimes God's promises don't materialize as soon as we would like, and we wonder if God has forgotten us.

What God has promised He is able to perform. Think of the many wonderful promises He has made. How do we know He is able to do what He has promised? Because He is the almighty God. As we wait for the fruition of God's promises, we can find confidence in knowing that God is not only in charge of the event, but He is in charge of the timing. What energizes us as we wait for Him is this thought: God has never promised anything to any of us that He is not able to do, and He is faithful to do what He has promised.

God will not prostitute His power to give us desires that will in the end be destructive to our walk with Him. But if we are consumed with a passion to find God's will through His Word and His Holy Spirit, we can always be in the place where God can shower down His power upon us.

PRAY FOR YOUR CHILDREN

The effective, fervent prayer of a righteous man avails much.

JAMES 5:16

If I had to reduce it to just one thing, I would pray for my child's personal relationship with the Lord Jesus, because if that's solid, most of the other stuff will settle in.

Some days I have felt so burdened for my family that I have spent my whole prayer time praying for my children, either out loud or in writing, making sure I said everything I wanted to say. And God has answered my prayers in a way that would take ten books to describe.

Perhaps your children are (or will be) scattered around the country or the world. Remember this: though you are separated by hundreds of miles, you can feel a sense of oneness in the presence of God, a sense of security that God will do what He has promised. Or your children may still live with or near you, but through prayer you can draw even closer to them than physical proximity allows.

Through prayer, righteous parents can change the course and direction of their family. The prayer of a righteous parent can put a child's heart into the hand of the Lord, who then directs it like a watercourse wherever He pleases.

David Jeremiah

LIVE FOR JESUS

Go out into the highways and hedges, and compel them to come in,
that my house may be filled.

LUKE 14:23

P urely as an illustration, suppose the Lord Jesus told you you've got one year left on earth. Do you think He would then tell you to spend your time stockpiling food? Hardly! I think He would say, "Friend, you've got one year left to go up and down the highways and the byways and the corridors of this land with the gospel of Jesus Christ, sharing Him as you never have before. Sell everything you've got to buy literature, and get it to those who don't know. Give everything you have so that by the time I come back at the end of this year, you will have touched every human being you could possibly touch with the message of Jesus Christ, the Lord of glory."

It's not my task or purpose to make people feel guilty. Every one of us knows we could be doing a better job of telling other people about our Lord. I'm not talking about buttonholing people and being obnoxious. That's not what we're supposed to do. I'm just talking about starting every day by praying, "Lord, today I'm going to live for You. If You bring someone across my path who needs You, help me to sense it, and help me to do the right thing."

THE INWARD MAN

*Even though our outward man is perishing, yet the inward
man is being renewed day by day.*

2 CORINTHIANS 4:16

It is easy in our world to lose touch with the value of the
inward man. Because we are an accomplishment-oriented
society, it is hard to "rank" the inward man on those scales
that our culture deems important. Therefore, in order to
feel significant, we focus on developing the outward things
that give us credibility in the eyes of others.

Paul said that the "outward man is perishing." No
amount of working on it is going to change that. How sad
it is to see people wanting to look youthful in their obituary
picture in the paper when they are as dead as everyone else!
But Paul had a different philosophy. He accepted the fact
that the outward man is perishing and the inward man is
going to live forever.

But how exactly do we demonstrate that we value the
inward man? How do we invest in that part of us we know is
most important? We have to go into the spiritual gymnasium
and work out with the inward man just as we would work out
with the outward man to build up muscles or lose weight.

Just as the outward body needs food, so the inward man
needs food, and the Bible tells us that food is God's Word.

David Jeremiah

TALK TO THE LORD ABOUT TROUBLES

The righteous cry out, and the LORD hears, and delivers them out of all their troubles.

PSALM 34:17

D avid testified, "This poor man cried out, and the Lord heard him, and saved him out of all his troubles." C. S. Lewis once wrote, "Down through the ages whenever men had a need of courage they would cry out, 'Billy Budd, help me' and nothing happened. But for 1900 years, whenever men have needed courage and have cried out, 'Lord Jesus, help me' something always happened."

I love the Hebrew definition of the word *trouble*. The word literally translates "hang-ups." It means to be inhibited, tied up and restricted. When we lay hold of Christ, we are freed from our "hang-ups."

Sound too simple? It is! Yet when I've counseled with so many Christians in deep trouble, I've asked them, "Have you talked to the Lord about this?" They looked at me with a blank stare. "You mean tell Him?" Yes. When you acknowledge the reliability of the One who is in charge of your life and then admit your fear, you have to appropriate the power He has promised to give you. You have to tell it to Jesus.

IN HIS STEPS

To this you were called, because Christ also suffered for us, leaving us an example, that you should follow His steps.

1 PETER 2:21

After supper one evening, we decided to stroll along the beach to the boardwalk, about twenty blocks away. I remember pointing out to the children that they ought to be careful where they walked. We were barefoot and could easily step on broken shells or those horrid jellyfish.

Since my gait is usually about twice as fast as anyone else's, I was walking out in front of the rest of the family. Suddenly I sensed that someone was immediately behind me. The crunch of feet, not my own, was audible, and I looked over my shoulder to see one small son stretching to put his feet in the very footprints I was leaving in the sand. I guess he felt that the only way he could be sure that he avoided broken shells, jellyfish, and crabs was to step exactly where his father was stepping.

What a lesson I learned that day! Sometimes as I walk through the debris of this world, I shudder to think of all the spiritual jellyfish, broken shells, and crabs that lie in the path. There is no certain way to avoid these pitfalls apart from the steps of our heavenly Leader.

David Jeremiah

LITTLE PICTURES

*God is able to make all grace abound toward you, that you, always having all
sufficiency in all things, may have an abundance for every good work.*

2 CORINTHIANS 9:8

An old widow was living in poverty and want. A young
man, hearing she was in need, went to visit her to see
if he could be of any help. The old lady complained bitterly
of her condition and remarked that her son in Australia was
doing very well. Her friend inquired, "Doesn't he do anything to help you?" She replied, "No, nothing. He writes to
me regularly once a month, but he sends me only some little
pictures with his letters." The young man asked to see the
pictures she had received. To his surprise, he found each of
them to be twenty-pound notes. The poor old lady did not
realize the value of this foreign currency, but had imagined
them to be mere pretty pictures.

She had lived in poverty and want, whereas she could
have had all the bodily comforts she desired and needed so
badly. We smile at the foolishness of the old woman, but how
many of us are like her, living as though we were paupers
instead of sons and daughters of the King?

WISDOM MULTIPLIED

The wisdom that is from above is first pure, then peaceable, gentle, willing to yield, full of mercy and good fruits, without partiality and without hypocrisy.

JAMES 3:17

Heavenly wisdom is continually coming from above, as evidenced in James's use of the present tense in 3:17. God's supply of wisdom never runs dry, but keeps coming to us to meet the demands of each hour (James 1:5). This wisdom is manifested through God's Son, made available through God's Holy Spirit, and written down in God's holy book, the Bible. The wise man is the man who has given himself to Jesus Christ and who, with the Spirit's help, keeps his intellect in submission to the will of God.

The comparison of heavenly and earthly wisdom is instructive. The world's wisdom results in "confusion" (v. 16), but God's wisdom always brings "peace" (v.18). The result of the world's wisdom is "every evil thing" (v. 16), but God's wisdom produces fruit. In the fruit of God's wisdom are the seeds of more fruit; the fruit of righteousness is sown in peace (v. 18). God's wisdom automatically multiplies.

David Jeremiah

GIVE ME SOULS!

My heart's desire and prayer to God . . . is that they may be saved.
ROMANS 10:1

A recent survey by Christian pollster George Barna found that only half (53 percent) of born-again Christians feel a sense of responsibility to tell others about their faith. Compare that with these quotes from earlier generations of believers:

"I cared not where or how I lived, or what hardships I went through, so that I could but gain souls for Christ."
—David Brainerd

"Lord, give me souls or take my soul."
—George Whitefield

"Here let me burn out for God."
—Henry Martyn, on the shores of India

"I am very tired, but must go on. . . . A fire is in my bones. . . . Oh God, what can I say? Souls! Souls! Souls! My heart hungers for souls!"
—General William Booth

"I would rather win souls than be the greatest king or emperor on earth. My one ambition in life is to win as many as possible."—R. A. Torrey

MARCH

I cried out to You, O Lord: I said, "You are my refuge;
my portion in the land of the living."

—PSALM 142:5

LIVING ON THE LIVING GOD

I cried out to You, O LORD: I said, "You are my refuge,
my portion in the land of the living."

PSALM 142:5

David would have agreed with the old preacher who said, "There's no living in the land of the living like living on the living God." That preacher was right. The land of the living is not a reference to eternity or heaven. It is a reference to living right now. The Bible is written for people who are living in the land of the living, not for people who dream of "pie in the sky by and by."

The land of the living is where you and I live every day. We rise and face the challenges that the living face, and God is our portion in that land. He does not remove us from the land where we live in order to help us. Rather, He joins us where we are—our private world, our family, our job, our church—to meet our needs. The God of David is our God, and He is still our refuge and our portion.

David Jeremiah

NEVER FAIL TO FORGIVE

Forgive us our debts, as we forgive our debtors.

MATTHEW 6:12

When I was a teenager, I disobediently took my father's car out for a joyride when he wasn't home. Unfortunately, I ended up running the car off a country road and into a ditch. I went to him and said, "Dad, I've got to tell you, I feel terrible about what I did. I was wrong, deceitful, dishonest. I knew better than to do that. I'm sorry, and I want to ask you to forgive me." He said, "You are forgiven—but you will pay for the car."

When I damaged my father's car, did I cease to be my father's son? No. But my relational forgiveness was in deep trouble. If you want to know oneness with the Lord in your daily relationship with Him, if you want to feel the reality of your forgiveness when you pray to God, don't hold grudges against others and fail to forgive them. You can't come to God and expect to enjoy His forgiveness of your sins when you have not confessed your own sin of unforgiveness and forgiven your brother. If you want to know the daily sense of your forgiveness in your walk with the Lord, then you must forgive those who have wronged you.

HOW TO FEAR GOD

Only fear the LORD, and serve Him in truth with all your heart; for consider what great things He has done for you.

1 SAMUEL 12:24

In July 1861, in an act declaring September 26 as a National Day of Prayer and Fasting, Abraham Lincoln wrote: "It is fit and becoming in all people, at all times, to acknowledge and revere the Supreme Government of God; to bow in humble submission to his chastisement; to confess and deplore their sins and transgressions in the full conviction that the fear of the Lord is the beginning of wisdom. . . ."

That may be one of the best summaries ever penned of what it means to "fear the Lord." Note the action words: "to acknowledge . . . revere . . . bow . . . confess and deplore." To fear the Lord means more than just one thing. Indeed, it is a phrase that gathers together a number of attitudes and actions. In short, when we fear the Lord, we recognize God's proper place as Creator over us, His creation. If someone followed us around for a week, what evidence would they see that we fear the Lord? Which would they hear most—grumbles or gratitude, complaints or compassion?

A nation that fears the Lord is one whose citizens fear the Lord. Plan a "Personal Day of Prayer and Fasting" soon— a day to reaffirm your own fear of the Lord.

AS YOUR SOUL PROSPERS

Beloved, I pray that you may prosper in all things and be in health,
just as your soul prospers.

3 JOHN V. 2

Verse 2 contains a revealing concept: prospering in all things as your soul prospers. As I was studying this verse, I began to wonder what it would be like if one Sunday everyone arrived at church in the same physical condition their souls were in. That is, our outward manifestation of "prosperity" would be in direct correlation to the prosperity of our souls. It might be a very interesting sight!

How would you arrive if that happened? In a wheelchair? On crutches? Would you need assistance getting in the door? Or would you arrive in fine shape, physically fit because your soul was in such fine condition? John knew that Gaius was a godly man, so he did not hesitate to pray that he prospered in all things in the same way his soul prospered.

If the church is going to accomplish all it is supposed to, we need many more vigorous workers than we have now. We need people who are willing, like Gaius, to play a supporting role, empowering others in their spiritual walk. The Bible promises spiritual blessings for those willing to work in such a way.

BLESSED ARE THOSE WHO TRUST IN THE LORD

Let us not grow weary while doing good, for in due season we shall reap if we do not lose heart.

GALATIANS 6:9

Blessed is the man who trusts in the Lord, and whose hope is the Lord. For he shall be like a tree planted by the waters, which spreads out its roots by the river, and will not fear when heat comes; but its leaf will be green, and will not be anxious in the year of drought, nor will cease from yielding fruit" (Jeremiah 17:7–8).

The person who loves God is like a tree with deep roots. During a drought, when all the other trees are perishing, that tree will remain healthy and strong. There is no anxiety, for the commitment of that tree reaches beyond the circumstances of the storm.

If we are to succeed in the midst of trouble, and if we are not to quit when the going gets tough, we need to get our roots down deep into the Lord, establishing a commitment in Christ that goes beyond our circumstances. As the apostle Paul put it, "And let us not grow weary while doing good, for in due season we shall reap if we do not lose heart" (Galatians 6:9).

David Jeremiah

WHEN IN DOUBT, DON'T!

Shall not the Judge of all the earth do right?

GENESIS 18:25

Everyone has doubted God's justice at times. We may not think of it that way; we may just wonder, "Why did God allow an event to happen that way?" I know I have wondered the same thing on many occasions.

I have learned to take many things in my Christian walk purely by faith. I have learned enough about God through Scripture and His faithfulness in my life that when I come to a place where I am tempted to doubt—I don't. I take by faith the fact that God is good, that the Judge of all the earth shall do right (Genesis 18:25). Not to have that core conviction governing one's thoughts daily is to live in a world of vacillation and shifting shadows.

If we do not live our lives based on the fact that God is righteous, we have no basis for righteousness in our own lives.

LOVED!

God is love.

1 JOHN 4:8

When Scottish teenager George Matheson learned he was losing his eyesight, he determined to finish his studies at the University of Glasgow as quickly as possible. Blindness overtook him while he pursued graduate studies for Christian ministry, but his family rallied to his side. His sisters even learned Greek and Hebrew to help him in his assignments.

The real blow came later, when his fiancée determined she just couldn't marry a blind man. Breaking the engagement, she returned the ring. George was devastated. Years later, when he was a beloved pastor in Scotland, his sister became engaged, and the news opened old wounds in his heart. More mature now, he turned to God and out of the experience wrote a prayer that later became a much-loved hymn:

> *O love that wilt not let me go,*
> *I rest my weary soul in thee;*
> *I give thee back the life I owe,*
> *That in thing ocean depths its flow*
> *May richer, fuller be.*

Have you been disappointed recently? God's love will never let you go, and in its continuous, compassionate, costly flow, your life will richer, fuller be.

David Jeremiah

WHAT WILL WE DO IN HEAVEN?

They sing . . . the song of the Lamb, saying: "Great and marvelous are your works, Lord God Almighty! Just and true are your ways, O king of the saints!"
REVELATION 15:3

We will never get bored! We will sing. Those who could never carry a tune on earth will be able to sing in heaven and never grow weary of exalting the name of the King of kings. We'll serve perfectly, enabled by the power that is able to conform all things to the pleasure of His sovereign will. We'll share unbroken fellowship with angels, members of the church, God the Father, Jesus, and the spirits of just men made perfect. Never again will we have to say good-bye to a loved one or give a farewell party. Through our resurrected bodies, we will have instant access to each other at all times.

God has different things for different people to do. God made each of us unique, with a special ministry and a responsibility. Each of us in our own right is peerless in what God has called us to do. There are many distinct groups in heaven, all unique in their responsibility before God.

When we get to heaven, we are going to praise God perfectly. All of heaven will be filled with music. Throughout eternity, worship will be our privileged occupation.

THE POWER OF ONE

What man of you, having a hundred sheep, if he loses one of them,
does not leave the ninety-nine in the wilderness, and go after the one
which is lost until he finds it?

LUKE 15:4

Jesus said that His purpose for coming into the world was to seek and to save that which was lost (Luke 19:10). It is at this point that Christianity is separate from all other religions of the world. Christianity is God searching for man. Christianity is the Shepherd looking for the sheep. How different it is! And how blessed we are to be part of it!

And how glad we are that Jesus didn't work on the basis of percentages. The shepherd had 99 percent of his flock safely at home. A modern businessman might have figured that the cost of finding the one wasn't worth the value of the sheep. *Take your losses and move on,* he might have thought. Yet the shepherd left the ninety-nine and went to find the one. The woman who lost the coin had 90 percent of her wealth. But the man with the lost son had only 50 percent of his. With God, the percentages don't matter, for every single one is important and worth finding.

David Jeremiah

THE SPIRIT AND THE WORD

Let the word of Christ dwell in you richly in all wisdom, teaching and admonishing one another in psalms and hymns and spiritual songs, singing with grace in your hearts to the Lord.

COLOSSIANS 3:16

Ephesians points to our being filled with the Spirit. Colossians points to our being filled with the Word of God, which dwells within us richly. Then, by psalms and hymns and spiritual songs, we partake in wisdom and teaching together. Combine the two passages and we see a melody and countermelody of being filled with God's Word and God's Spirit, responding with beautiful music in both cases.

We need both of these, the Spirit and the Word, to be Christians. Subtract either and it's simply not possible. One reshapes the heart and the other the mind, and together they make us whole persons molded to the image of Christ. The Word of God provides the content; the Spirit of God applies it. He impresses the teachings of the Scriptures upon us, applies them to us, and reminds us of them at need. Throughout time, many believers have been inspired to create hymns as they've read God's Word. Very often, they've said they were convinced that God gave them the melody as well. How could powerful songs like "Amazing Grace" and "Joy to the World" have any other source but God?

PEACE IN THE STORM

He calms the storm, so that its waves are still.

PSALM 107:29

Remember the story in the Gospels about Jesus and the disciples in a boat on the Sea of Galilee (Matthew 8:23–27)? A fierce storm arose, and the disciples were certain they were about to perish. The disciples learned a great lesson that day, one that could only be taught in a storm—not in a classroom. Jesus had gone to the back of the boat to take a nap, and a huge storm blew up. Their fear is most evident in Luke's account: "Master, Master, we are perishing!" (8:24). It would appear they didn't make the connection immediately that riding in the boat with them was the One who created the wind and the waves. Perhaps it did click with them, and that's why they woke Jesus up and were chastised by Him for their "little faith."

But we can understand how they felt because it's how we feel when the storms of our lives come up. We forget that we know the very One who allowed the storm in the first place and that He can cause it to stop or see us through it.

David Jeremiah

DEVELOP A SPIRITUAL
IMMUNE SYSTEM

How can a young man cleanse his way? By taking heed according to Your word.
PSALM 119:9

One of the things I've learned a lot about in the last few years is the immune system. Our God-given immune systems help us fight off the forces that would destroy our bodies. If our immune systems are functioning at 100 percent, we don't have to take medicines because they will just fight off the disease seeking to take over our bodies. But if our immune systems aren't healthy, then we become susceptible to lots of things. If we get to the condition of an AIDS patient, our bodies lose their ability to fight off almost anything. To fight off sickness, we have to strengthen the body's immune system. That may mean stopping some things we enjoy doing and starting some things we haven't been doing. It's a matter of critical importance.

The same is true spiritually. In order to increase our immunity to sin, we must strengthen ourselves through prayer, the Word, and fellowship with other strong Christians.

THE TRUTH ABOUT MERCY

Through the LORD's mercies we are not consumed, because His compassions fail not. They are new every morning; great is Your faithfulness.

LAMENTATIONS 3:22—23

When Thomas Chisholm wrote the words to the song "Great Is Thy Faithfulness," he made a tiny error. The song is based on this Scripture. He wrote, "Morning by morning, new mercies I see." But the point of this passage is that the prophet Jeremiah did not see any new mercies. He didn't see a thing. He had no visible evidence of God's mercies at all. Morning by morning brought horror and pain and dread—not new mercies. Jeremiah was not saying, "I trust You because I understand everything that is going on in my life." He was saying, "I trust You because You are God and You cannot fail. And I know You cannot lie."

There are times when life is not easy, when it is hard to believe in the faithfulness of God. We try to hold on and find out what God is up to, and sometimes He seems to have disappeared. And we listen to the words of the enemy, who tries to pull us away from what we know and cause us to operate on how we feel.

God is faithful whether you feel like He is or not, whether you think He is or not, whether you observe His faithfulness or not. God, who cannot lie, is faithful.

David Jeremiah

DEPENDING ON GOD

Our God . . . will deliver us from your hand, O king. But if not, let it be known to you, O king, that we do not serve your gods.

DANIEL 3:17–18

I don't care how strong a Christian you are; peer pressure today is so intense that you cannot cope with it apart from the Lord. If you don't depend on God with all of your heart, if you don't ask God to give you the strength you need to stand up and be counted, and if you don't realize that He is your ally and goes with you every day, you cannot possibly make it through these years without the risk of ruining your life.

Three young men from the book of Daniel (chapter 3)—Shadrach, Meshach, and Abed-Nego—are models for depending upon God when the heat is on. When everyone in Babylon was bowing down to the king's idol (including, apparently, the rest of the Jewish captives), these three refused. One way to get noticed in a crowd is to remain standing when everyone else is bowing on their knees!

Their dependence was on God alone, and He delivered them. Every person who walks with God must be prepared to depend on Him when the pressure comes to conform.

TRIALS VS. TEMPTATIONS

No temptation has overtaken you except such is common to man; but God is faithful, who will not allow you to be tempted beyond what you are able.

1 CORINTHIANS 10:13

A consumer protection group will test a car to find its flaws, while the car manufacturer tests a car to find its strengths. In the same way, Satan tempts us to bring out the bad (James 1:13–18), while God tests us to bring out the good (vv. 1:1–12). Nothing tests the integrity of our faith like our response to temptation.

When we hear of people falling prey to temptation, we are not surprised. But when we face temptation ourselves, we are often shocked. We shouldn't be surprised, for temptation is inevitable. The more we grow toward the Lord, the more we are tempted.

Unless we acknowledge the reality of temptation, we have set ourselves up to fail. Paul agrees with James that temptation should not be considered unusual in the life of a Christian but common to every believer.

David Jeremiah

OPPORTUNITIES

May the God of all grace, who called us to His eternal glory by Christ Jesus, after you have suffered a while, perfect, establish, strengthen, and settle you.

1 PETER 5:10

P roblems are often given to us by God to provide us greater opportunities. As God's children, we need to learn how to look for the possibilities in our problems. God's people have always worked this way. An entire section of Scripture, the "prison epistles," was written while Paul was incarcerated in a Roman jail cell. The book of Revelation was written by John while he was exiled on the isle of Patmos. It was in prison that John Bunyan saw the great allegory that would later become the immortal *Pilgrim's Progress*. Sometimes good things come from bad times.

Joseph learned from his prison experience that he was not forgotten by God. As a matter of fact, God used a relationship formed while Joseph was in prison to accomplish His plan.

I remember hearing Charles Colson say that his lowest times as a believer have been far more fulfilling that all his glory days in the White House when he was an unbeliever. During the lonely days of prison, he learned to know God. Sometimes loneliness and difficulties are necessary in our lives, because the problems are the means God uses to provide opportunities for us.

CONFIDENCE IN GOD'S PRESENCE

The LORD, He is the One who goes before you. He will be with you,
He will not leave you nor forsake you; do not fear nor be dismayed.

DEUTERONOMY 31:8

When Susanna Wesley was on her deathbed, she gathered her children around her. As she was about to be called home to heaven, she admonished them not to weep but rather to "sing a hymn of praise." Then with her last breath, she reminded them that the greatest comfort we have in any circumstance is the fact that "God is with us."

We often need that reminder! It is especially reassuring to hear these words when God has given us a difficult assignment, one that seems impossible and for which we feel totally unqualified. We are not the first to have experienced fear and hesitation in accepting God's assignment.

Moses certainly didn't do any cartwheels when God asked him to lead the Israelites out of Egypt. He was not excited about the task because he felt ill equipped to accomplish it. That's when God spoke these courage-infusing words: "I will certainly be with you" (Exodus 3:12).

Those few precious words remind us that with God's presence and help, we can accomplish any assignment. His presence instills confidence in our hearts.

David Jeremiah

THE BEST VIOLINS

We also glory in tribulations, knowing that tribulation produces perseverance; and perseverance, character; and character, hope.

ROMANS 5:3–4

An old violin maker was much envied by fellow artisans because of the superior quality of the instruments he produced. He finally disclosed the secret of his success. He said that while the others went into the protected valleys to cut wood to make their violins, he climbed the rugged crags of a nearby mountain in order to secure trees that had become severely twisted and gnarled by storms. From these weather-beaten monarchs of the forest he then fabricated his violins—famous for their tone and beauty.

He knew that the fierce trials of the mountain gales caused such trees to strengthen and toughen their fibers. It was this—their storm-tortured heart and grain—that produced the deep, colorful sound when the instrument was played. Likewise, the Lord allows sore difficulties to come into our lives that we may more fully bring forth the music of His grace when our soul-trying experiences have done their sanctifying work.

NOT BY SIGHT

Trust in the LORD with all your heart, and lean not on your own understanding; in all your ways acknowledge Him, and He shall direct your paths.

PROVERBS 3:5–6

At the beginning of flight training, a student flies with an instructor by his side, over familiar terrain, and in perfect weather. All his decisions are based on sight. But at the end, when a student pilot receives his "instrument rating," he has learned to fly by himself, over unfamiliar terrain, and in total darkness. He has learned to trust not his sight but his instruments—compass, altimeter, air speed, and radar. He has learned to "fly blind."

Just as a flight instructor's ultimate goal is to see a student get his instrument rating, so the father in Proverbs had the same goal for his son. What is the spiritual equivalent of an instrument rating? It is trusting in the Lord, not in one's own understanding. Every parent, teacher, and leader knows his protégés will one day encounter darkness, storms, and unfamiliar terrain in life. The key to their graduation and promotion is learning to live by faith, not by sight (2 Corinthians 5:7).

"Flying blind" in life doesn't mean closing your eyes; it means keeping them on the Lord.

David Jeremiah

THE PURSUIT OF HAPPINESS

[Jesus] opened His mouth and taught them, saying, "Blessed are the poor in spirit, for theirs is the kingdom of heaven."

MATTHEW 5:2–3

Malcolm Muggeridge once called the pursuit of happiness the most disastrous purpose set before mankind, something slipped into the Declaration after "life and liberty" at the last moment, almost by accident. In his *Screwtape Letters*, C. S. Lewis had the archdevil, Screwtape, advise his apprentice demons on the lure of happiness. He called it "an ever-increasing craving for an ever-diminishing pleasure." That's exactly how the pursuit of happiness works in this world.

Pleasure is an anesthesia for deadening the pain of empty lives. There seem to be few happy people around today. That's why I appreciate the words of Jesus in the Sermon on the Mount. Nine different times Jesus uses the word *blessed*, which roughly translates to "happy." The core values Jesus offers in the Beatitudes describe life that is really worth living.

BREAK OUT IN PRAISE

Praise the LORD, for the LORD is good; sing praises to His name, for it is pleasant.

PSALM 135:3

Praise and worship are *refining* processes. We can't be in God's presence without a deep awareness of our sin and without confessing and allowing the purification that only He can provide. Worship cleanses our hands and hearts, and then we can see how to fight. Then we can clear the sinful mists from our eyes and do things God's way.

Some have said that Satan has an allergic reaction whenever there is true worship. That's an interesting way of visualizing it; perhaps when we break out in praise, the devil breaks out in hives. I don't know whether he itches, sneezes, or coughs, but I do know he becomes very uncomfortable on those occasions when we take our eyes off ourselves and place them squarely and worshipfully on the Lord of grace. That's when God's mighty works finally come to pass. That's when we take powerful weapons in hand, crying, "Onward, Christian soldiers!" and advancing on the enemy's holdings. The forces of hell cannot prevail against the uplifted name of Christ.

David Jeremiah

THE SECRET TO STORMS

They are glad because [the storms] are quiet; so He guides them to their desired haven.

PSALM 107:30

God's purposes in the storms you encounter are always to guide you to a haven. Think about it: we don't just go out on the sea to sit there; we go for a purpose. If a storm interrupts that purpose, God will direct you through it, or He may change the purpose of your trip altogether.

I have learned this about storms: the place you thought you wanted to go heading into the storm is not always the place you think you want to go coming out of the storm. Sometimes storms can change your mind about things you thought you wanted.

The secret to experiencing these changes is starting the journey with a receptive heart. If you head into a storm saying, "Thy will be done," then your will and God's will become one.

DELIVERANCE FROM POVERTY

Behold, the eye of the LORD is on those who fear Him, on those who hope in His mercy, to deliver their soul from death, and to keep them alive in famine.

PSALM 33:18–19

David gives us permission to pray for deliverance from poverty and need. This psalm talks about being kept alive in times of deprivation. God loves to deliver His people from that condition. We are always aware of those who are struggling materially and wonder how they are going to make it. God can deliver them from it.

I talk with Christian people all the time who are in the midst of great need. I always ask them, "Have you asked God pointedly, naming the details of this situation, to help you and deliver you from it?" They have often prayed in generalities, but not in specifics.

My friend, when you are in the lions' den, you need to pray about the lion—by name!

UNCHANGEABLE PERSONALITY

For I am the LORD, I do not change.

MALACHI 3:6

I f you have kids, have you ever noticed how they work you? Another word for this is manipulation. They live in the same house with you, so they study you. They know when you're in a certain kind of mood and when they should move in. If they see you're troubled or upset over something, they know it's not the time to make a request. If you've had a great day, they make their move.

You don't have to work God. He's always in a good mood. He's always the same. You don't have to sneak up on God when you think it is appropriate to ask Him for what you need. And that affects your fellowship with Him and your attitude toward Him. He loves you, and He wants to do as much for you as He can at any given time. It doesn't matter when you call. He's always there.

WORDS OF LIFE

Pleasant words are like a honeycomb, sweetness to the soul and health to the bones.

PROVERBS 16:24

K arl Marx devoted his entire life to writing about the demise of capitalism and the coming of communism. He, along with Friedrich Engels, wrote one of the most well-known political treatises in all of history, the *Communist Manifesto*. As evidence of his keen understanding of the great power of words, Marx is credited with saying: "Give me twenty-six lead soldiers and I will conquer the world!" Who are the twenty-six lead soldiers Marx referred to? They are the twenty-six letters of the alphabet on a printing press.

All words have power and meaning (Isaiah 55:11). Jesus said we would be held accountable for even our idle words (Matthew 12:36–37), and Proverbs says that words have the power of life and death (18:21). So the question is not whether words have power. The question is, "What power am I releasing with my words?" If you have sent forth words that hurt, take them back with an apology and replace them with words that heal. The greatest untapped source of heal-ing in life is "pleasant words." You may not consider yourself a physician, but you should—as long as you are dispensing words of life.

David Jeremiah

CHANGE YOUR THINKING

Every good gift and every perfect gift is from above, and comes down from the Father of lights, with whom there is no variation or shadow of turning.

JAMES 1:17

In contrast to the evil enticements that come from within us, every good gift comes from God, who is over us. The text literally says that such benefits come down to us in a steady stream from the Father of lights.

God's nature is unchanging. He will forever be both good and trustworthy. Jesus (Matthew 6:30; 7:11) and Paul (Romans 13:14) shared the same perspective. James might add to Paul's words that the believer should not only refrain from thinking about gratifying his desires, but also avoid thinking about *not* gratifying his desires.

We are not to grit our teeth and make up our mind that we will not do a certain thing. The key to dealing with temptation is to fill our minds with other things. Since temptation begins with our thoughts, changing what we think about is the key to victory.

LOVE AUTHENTICALLY

Husbands, love your wives, just as Christ also loved the church and gave Himself for her.

EPHESIANS 5:25

Christ loved the church with an authentic love. By that, I mean it was real. It wasn't fantasy; it was the church as the church is. It was you and me as we were and as we are. Christ was under no illusion when He sought us in love. And of course, that is the way husbands are to love their wives— with realistic, authentic love.

We must recognize that our love will embrace all of our wife's faults and failures and all of her unlovable and disagreeable elements. When a young couple enters into marriage with unrealistic expectations, it doesn't take long before those expectations are brought back down to earth. Marriage is a mixture of ideals and reality. It's a wonderful thing to know that Christ loves us as we were and continues to love us as we are. He loves us in spite of our sins.

Christ's love for us is not idealized, romanticized, or stylized. It is simply authentic, meeting sinners like us exactly where we are.

David Jeremiah

STAND, NO MATTER WHAT

Stand fast in one spirit, with one mind striving together for faith of the gospel.
PHILIPPIANS 1:27

Someone has said that a man who refuses to stand for something will sooner or later fall for anything. Because of his stand for the faith, Paul was facing the possibility of death, and he was willing to pay the supreme price if called upon to do so.

In writing to the Philippian believers, he shared his concern about their willingness to stand against the pressure of persecution. He hoped that he might be with them in person to encourage them if such a thing occurred, but he had no guarantee. So he sent them a strategy that would serve them well, even if he was not available to personally cheer them on.

Paul's game plan for the Philippians is needed in our day too. We are in the minority, surrounded by the enemy, and constantly being undermined by members of our own army. Many among God's people have adopted a philosophy that gives to survival the attributes of victory. But in our day, as in Paul's, anything short of victory is just the postponement of defeat!

PREACHING CHRIST CRUCIFIED

Then Philip went down to the city of Samaria and preached Christ to them.
ACTS 8:5

Notice what Philip preached when he arrived in Samaria: Christ! What did that mean in the first century? Remember, they didn't have the New Testament to use. All they had was the Old Testament. So when Philip "preached Christ to them" (Acts 8:5), he was simply explaining how Jesus Christ fulfilled the Old Testament expectation of the coming Jewish Messiah. The only message the early church had was the birth, life, death, and resurrection of Jesus of Nazareth. "Christ and Him crucified" was the message (1 Corinthians 2:2).

The church today has so muddied the gospel water that we can preach forever and never get around to Christ crucified. We've added cultural issues and social issues and theological issues to the gospel that probably would have just confused the first-century Christians. They only had an eyewitness story to tell of a Messiah who died and rose again. That was what Christ did, and that is what the church preached.

And look what happened when Philip preached that simple message. Multitudes of people responded to his preaching and the miracles he performed, "and there was great joy in that city" (Acts 8:6–8).

David Jeremiah

USE IT OR LOSE IT

Therefore take the talent from him, and give it to him who has ten talents.

MATTHEW 25:28

Each believer has talents given by God that we are to use for His glory. We can't claim that we have no gifts or that we have been given no opportunity. The fact is, what we do with what we have will be the basis of our judgment. I won't be judged on my inability to sing or play the piano, but I will have to give an account of the gifts that I have.

If we don't use our talent for God, we will lose it. It doesn't remain dormant. It won't remain hidden. We will end up not having the opportunity we had at the beginning. On the other hand, if we are faithful in the use of our abilities, God will multiply our opportunities for service. The way to grow in influence and service is to use what we already have—then the Lord will reward us with more opportunity.

Remember, someday we will have to give an account at the judgment seat of Christ. As Christians, we won't be judged for our sins—they have already been forgiven. But we will be judged for the stewardship of those things God has given us. We'll be judged on quality, not quantity. We have been given incredible potential for serving God. How are we putting ours to use?

TRUE HAPPINESS

Blessed are the pure in heart, for they shall see God.

MATTHEW 5:8

B*lessed* means "happy, blissful, joyous, ecstatic." Those characteristics the Lord lists are like an explosion on His lips, a description of the inner joy we can experience. This expression was commonly seen in the book of Psalms. "Blessed is the man who walks not in the counsel of the ungodly," says Psalm 1:1. Anyone who has ever been burned by ungodly counsel will attest to the fact that a man who doesn't get mixed up with ungodly counsel is happy. "Blessed is he whose transgression is forgiven," we read in Psalm 32:1. We are to be blissful and ecstatic over the fact that the Lord has taken away our sins. That's the same expression Christ used when He began talking about the Christian life. *Blissful, happy, joyous*—these are the words that describe the Christian walk.

Matthew 5:1–12 describes nine characteristics of the happy Christian life. If you want to know what happiness is all about, search through this "happiness manifesto" from the Lord Jesus. He'll explain to you what true happiness is all about.

David Jeremiah

APRIL

～

I am not alone, but I am with the Father who sent me.

—John 8:16

BEWARE FOOLISH FRIENDS

*He who walks with wise men will be wise, but the companion
of fools will be destroyed.*

PROVERBS 13:20

I t is important not to choose fools for friends because you
will become just like them: "He who walks with wise men
will be wise, but the companion of fools will be destroyed."
This is important for young people to know, especially during the years when peer pressure is so great. Christians are
not supposed to live like isolationists, walling ourselves
off from those who need Christ. It is fine to have casual
friendships with those who are not wise, but not committed
friendships. It is when we begin to open ourselves up to others on a committed level that we are likely to be influenced
to become like them.

Sometimes Christians forge friendships with unwise
people thinking they can change them. But you will both
be changed. Many Christian young people marry non-
Christians thinking they can win them over after the
marriage. It rarely happens. Everyone is on their best behavior during courtship, and after marriage, the mountain
of unbelief looms larger than it did before. You shouldn't
make committed friendships with fools, but you should look
for faithful friends.

David Jeremiah

A NOTE OF VICTORY

Oh, sing to the LORD a new song! For He has done marvelous things;
His right hand and His holy arm have gained Him the victory.

PSALM 98:1

Did you know there is someone who really gets bent out of shape whenever you go to church? No, not that fellow in the next pew who objects to your singing. It truly torments the devil and every one of his "assistants" when you worship God, in the public sanctuary or the private one. It throws a wrench into the detailed agenda of demonic works. In all the other things we do, from watching television to grocery shopping to taking business trips, there are countless windows of opportunity for the devil to steal in and do his thing. But when you worship God devotedly, Satan is out of his league. He is completely stripped of power, and that's always been the one thing the devil can't abide.

Worship has always been our weapon. Consider that midnight in a Philippian jail, when two prisoners named Paul and Silas lifted their voices and sang praises to God. Think of all the psalms in which David begins in deep depression, lamenting the injustice of his enemies' success. In so many of these, he turns his attention and poetry to the praises of God, and his psalm finishes on a note of victory. That can become the pattern in your life.

TAKE HOPE IN THE RISEN CHRIST

Blessed be the God and Father of our Lord Jesus Christ, who according to His abundant mercy has begotten us again to a living hope through the resurrection of Jesus Christ.

1 PETER 1:3

The resurrection of our Lord is the single greatest event in history. Had the Lord merely died, He would have been considered a great teacher and a moral leader, but He would not have proven Himself God. By coming out of the grave, He triumphed over death and hell, showed His sacrifice on the cross as being acceptable to God, and gave hope of eternal life to everyone who puts their trust in Him.

Every other religious leader lies buried in the earth. Mohammed lies dead and buried. Buddha, Confucius, Zoroaster, and all the others who have attempted to lead men and women into a religious experience apart from Almighty God could not defeat death. But Jesus Christ, in what is one of the best documented facts in history, rose victorious from the grave. In this troubled world today, we can take hope in the risen Christ.

David Jeremiah

HE IS SOVEREIGN

Yours is the kingdom and the power and the glory forever.

MATTHEW 6:13

A critic might suggest that, given the state of the world, Christ the King is not doing a very good job running His kingdom. But please understand that one day Christ will institute His kingdom over the kingdom of this world, and He will rule and reign and bring order our of the earth's present chaos. You may think that your personal life is a mirror of the world—out of control, headed for calamity. Just when I think things are rolling along smoothly and in control, something will happen that I never could have dreamed of. Out of order comes chaos! But what a wonderful thing it is to go to God in prayer, knowing that He is sovereign over my life. And not only my life, but all creation.

Sometimes God allows us to sense in a practical way that everything is on track and under control. That's just one of His blessings—icing on the cake, so to speak. Those are special times. But it's when we don't have that sense, when we don't have evidence our eyes can see, that we need to remember this prayer: "Yours is the kingdom!"

A RISEN KING!

But the angel answered and said to the women, "Do not be afraid, for I know that you seek Jesus who was crucified. He is not here; for He is risen, as He said."

MATTHEW 28:5–6

Every year, people climb a mountain in the Italian Alps and stand at an outdoor crucifix. There they remember that the Lord Jesus died. A tourist noticed that a little trail led off from the shrine of the cross. He made his way down the trail, and to his surprise, he found another shrine overgrown with brush. This shrine symbolized the empty tomb. Unfortunately, it had been neglected. Reflecting on the experience, the tourist said it reminded him of many Christians who stop at the cross and never proceed to the empty tomb.

If we make our final stop at the cross, we miss the core of Christianity. Without the resurrection, our faith is dead. Because Christ rose from the dead, our past is forgiven and our future is secure. The empty tomb represents victory for every Christian.

Especially at Easter, we need to take time to reflect on the meaning of the resurrection. For the Christian, the resurrection is a cause for great celebration!

David Jeremiah

TO HELP US GROW

The testing of your faith produces patience. But let patience have its perfect work, that you may be perfect and complete, lacking nothing.

JAMES 1:3–4

In order to use us, God sets in motion a plan for shaping us into the kind of people He wants us to be. Sometimes that means we experience awful pain, giving up what we want to keep and going forward into areas we'd rather leave unexplored. But if we are going to be used by the Lord for His purposes, that process has to take place. That's exactly what happened to Joseph. As a favored young man, beloved and chosen by his father as his heir, Joseph was unexpectedly dropped into a pit. Before he knew what was happening, he was a family slave in a foreign country, serving under a hard man. If ever a man had reason to be bitter, it was Joseph.

But the wonderful thing is that Joseph did *not* become bitter. He was able to dream, to recognize the fact that God was shaping him for ministry—using the tough times of his life to prepare him for something great. All of us go through trying times, and they don't happen by accident. God arranges those times to help us grow.

I JUST KNOW

If a man dies, shall he live again?

JOB 14:14

Four hundred years before Christ's birth, the Greek philosopher Socrates lay dying from poison. He was considered the wisest teacher in the world, but when his friends asked, "Shall we live again?" he could only answer, "I hope so, but no man can know."

In Job 14:14, another man asked the same question: "If a man dies, shall he live again?" It's an age-old question. It haunts many people and tests every religious persuasion—the most crucial question of the ages. In Hebrews 2:15, we find that some men live all their lives in bondage to the fear of death. Many are afraid that death will catch up with them. Without some assurance of life after death, death becomes a terrifying proposition. But that is exactly why we can celebrate Easter: the resurrection of Jesus Christ answers that age-old question once and for all. The resurrection takes Christianity out of the realm of philosophy and turns it into a fact of history. It proves that there is life beyond this life.

David Jeremiah

A Gracious Offer

Be blameless and harmless . . . in the midst of a crooked and perverse nation, among whom ye shine as lights in the world, holding forth the word of life.

PHILIPPIANS 2:15–16 KJV

When we "shine as lights" in the world, the testimony of our personal holiness makes an impact on those around us. But the testimony of a righteous lifestyle is incomplete if there is no explanation to accompany it. I never have believed too much in the power of the "silent" witness. But when a godly life is accompanied by the presentation of the Word of Life, the effect can be dramatic.

The Word of Life is the total message of God's Word. It not only brings life to those who are dead in their sins, but it also sustains life each day for the disciple who is nurtured by it. When we are told to "hold it forth," the word that is used is one that was often chosen to describe a host offering wine to a guest at a banquet. It is the picture of a gracious offer of the gospel of Jesus Christ to those who do not know Him.

COMFORT IN HIS FATHER

I am not alone, but I am with the Father who sent Me.

JOHN 8:16

Although Jesus walked alone in His mission, suffered alone, was rejected by the world, and was denied by His friends, our lonely Savior had consolation. His heavenly Father was with Him: "And yet if I do judge, My judgment is true; for I am not alone, but I am with the Father who sent Me" (John 8:16).

Even though Jesus might have felt alone at times like we do, He knew He had a Father in heaven who would be with Him: "And He who sent Me is with Me. The Father has not left Me alone, for I always do those things that please Him" (v. 29).

Christ promises that people can find peace in Him: "Come to Me, all you who labor and are heavy laden, and I will give you rest" (Matthew 11:28).

Our Savior promises that He can relieve people's burdens, even the burden of loneliness. He has conquered loneliness for us by His death on the cross.

David Jeremiah

LIVE ABOVE DECEPTION

I am the way, the truth, and the life. No one comes to the
Father except through Me.

JOHN 14:6

In John 14:6, Jesus said, "I am the way, the truth and the life. No one comes to the Father except through Me." Jesus is the truth. God accomplishes His will on earth through truth, and Satan accomplishes his purposes on earth through lies. When the child of God believes the truth, then the Spirit of God can work in him, God's Word can work in him, and he can be set free from deception.

But when we play with the deceptive words of Satan and allow that deception into our hearts, we open the door for him to wreak havoc in our lives and in the lives of our families. Every time there is destruction among God's people, it's because the deceiver has been allowed to have just a little bit of a foothold in someone's life.

Today, the spirit of deception is rampant. But let's not forget that in the midst of this problem, there is Jesus. In the midst of the deception, there is the Truth. In the midst of all of the seduction of our society, there is the absolute, rock-solid person of the Lord Jesus Christ—the Way, the Truth, and the Life. When we put our trust in Him, we can live above deception and on the level of truth.

TRUE JOY

Let them shout for joy and be glad, who favor my righteous cause.

PSALM 35:27

I read a quote once from a man who said, "I think I must be the happiest man in the world! I have never met anyone who has had as much fun as I have had." The words were not spoken by a playboy or a globetrotter or an adventurer. They were spoken by a Christian missionary by the name of Frank Laubach, whose life was dedicated to the cultivation of literacy among the backward people of the world. He never went searching for happiness—he just found it as a by-product of his search for something more important.

Dr. Laubach described delighted men and women weeping for joy when they discovered how to read. "No other work in the world could possibly have brought me so much happiness," he said. He didn't live with prosperity or worldly success, but he found happiness. True joy is a by-product, not a goal.

David Jeremiah

TAKE THE POWER OF THE LORD

Thou art holy, O thou that inhabitest the praises of Israel.

PSALM 22:3 KJV

When we go forth into the battle—whether we battle through a family crisis or a career problem—we have two strategies. We can go in our own weakness and face defeat, or we can go in the power of the Lord. How do we do the latter? We simply love, adore, worship, and praise His name. We know that God makes His home in our praises, and He will march with us even to the farthest corners of the earth and the end of the age. As we worship, our life strategies come together in ways we could never have formulated on our own. Then, as we face the challenges head-on, we keep right on praising, right on singing to the Lord, who is greater and stronger any challenge that might stand in our path. The wonder of worship, guiding our everyday experiences, will totally change the way we see everything that confronts us.

What is that challenge for you today? I would urge you to focus not on the misery of the crisis, but on the mastery of Christ. Then follow Him into battle. See if the demons themselves don't turn and flee from the gateway, terrified by the sounds of godly praise and adoration.

COME OUT OF THE GRAVE

*It was necessary for the Christ to suffer and to rise from the dead the third day,
and that repentance and remission of sins should be preached in His name.*

LUKE 24:46–47

History is replete with those who have had delusions of grandeur about themselves. Some have even been willing to die for their cause. But, like all men, they were defeated by death. If we dug up their graves, we'd find their dead bodies. But that's what makes Jesus unique. He predicted His death, predicted His burial, and prophesied that one day He would come out of the grave victorious over death. Three days after His death, He did just that.

The Scriptures record it. All who have tried to disprove it have been defeated. Scientists, determined to destroy the Christian faith, have been unable, and many skeptics and atheists have been brought to faith after studying the death and resurrection of Jesus Christ. It is one of the most thoroughly documented events in the world's history.

Through His death we are redeemed, and through His blood our sin atoned, but all of that is meaningless if he did not come out of the grave. Christ's resurrection validated what He did on the cross.

David Jeremiah

FAITHFUL OVER FEW, RULER OVER MANY

Well done, good and faithful servant; you were faithful over a few things, I will make you ruler over many things.

MATTHEW 25:21

God owns everything and has decided to put some of it into our hands to manage. When the Lord looks down and sees an individual doing a good job administering a few things, He decides to put that individual in charge of a few more things. God evaluates our steward ship on the basis of how well we administer it, keeping His priorities in mind rather than our own. When He sees someone serving faithfully, He expands the responsibility, giving something else to be managed. But when He sees someone who manages God's resources based on a personal agenda, or who forgets to reflect the Spirit of God in his management, the Lord can choose to withhold any further responsibility.

That's why Jesus, in explaining the parable of the talents in Matthew 25:21, said, "Well done, good and faithful servant; you were faithful over a few things, I will make you ruler over many things."

NO GRUMBLING

Righteous lips are the delight of kings, and they love him who speaks what is right.
PROVERBS 16:13

L est you think you will never be called to speak before the ruler of the land, remember that you do so at least once every year—on April 15. You communicate in writing, validated by your signature, certain things about your financial status over the previous year. It is your responsibility to communicate that information honestly and righteously and without grumbling.

A pastor friend of mine paid no taxes for many years because his salary was so low, and he told me how resentful he was the first year he had to pay income taxes. The first few years he even addressed his envelope on April 15 to the "Infernal Revenue Service" or the "Eternal Revenue Service." But he soon realized that he was not speaking righteously before the king, and changed his attitude. It is our privilege as citizens to try to change the system through proper channels, but until it is changed we are to have "righteous lips" before the king.

David Jeremiah

WHAT'S MISSING?

Faith is the substance of things hoped for, the evidence of things not seen.
HEBREWS 11:1

In a day of material prosperity, when it seems that we have no lack of anything, there is one thing we are missing: heroes. Too often, those we traditionally look to as heroes end up being tarnished in some way—leaving us to search again.

Some people are designated as heroes during their lifetimes for achieving great things. But those enshrined in Hebrews 11 are remembered for their faith—faith by which they changed the world of their day. The most compelling thing about the people listed in Hebrews 11 is that they were ordinary people—people like you and me. The only thing they had going for them is the same thing available to us: faith.

INVESTING IN OUR CHILDREN

Only take heed to yourself, and diligently keep yourself, lest you forget the things your eyes have seen. . . . And teach them to your children and your grandchildren.

DEUTERONOMY 4:9

The values that we instill in our children are the values by which they will raise their families. And so the life of our investment is not just one generation, it is generation after generation. The key issue is not only what our children are now, but what they will become after internalizing the values we have passed on to them. And the clearest evidence of what they have internalized is what they pass on to their own children. A parent's influence on his child will have a long-term, lasting impact. Just as a seed takes time to germinate in the ground and bring forth fruit, so our teaching and influence on our children takes time to bear fruit as well. But it will bear fruit, for better or for worse.

The parent who wonders if the stress and strain of raising children—going against the flow of the culture, teaching them biblical values, spending the necessary time and money to give them the best opportunities—is really worth it need only remember the law of deposit and return. That which is sown today will bear fruit in the years to come.

David Jeremiah

SPIRITUAL ASPIRIN

The joy of the LORD is your strength.

NEHEMIAH 8:10

Doctors speak of the "threshold of pain," the level of awareness at which a person feels pain. Some people have a high threshold; others have a very low threshold. When you take an aspirin, it has no effect on your physical problem. All it does is raise your pain threshold so that you must experience more pain before you are aware of it. The aspirin makes you feel better because you don't feel how bad you feel.

Joy is like that. Happiness and joy are spiritual aspirin. When you are filled with the joy of the Lord, the hurts around you don't touch you so quickly.

I have found that music raises my threshold of psychological pain. On days when I am discouraged, I'll go home, turn on the stereo, and begin to listen to music. God uses that to assuage my soul and bring me out of pain. Is it any wonder that Saul required David to come and play for him on the harp to bring him out of his depression? That's what music can do in our hearts.

CHRISTIAN, NEVER GIVE UP!

I press toward the goal for the prize of the upward call of God in Christ Jesus.
PHILIPPIANS 3:14

In one of many attempts to scale Mount Everest before the successful climb in 1953, a team of mountain climbers made a final dash for the summit. Their courageous attempt failed and today they lie buried somewhere in the eternal snow. One of the party, who had stayed below when the final ascent was attempted, returned to London. One day as he was giving a lecture on mountain climbing, he stood before a magnificent picture of Mount Everest. As he concluded his address, he turned around and addressing the mountain, he said, "We have tried to conquer you and failed; we tried again and you beat us; but we shall beat you, for you cannot grow bigger, but we can."

Just as a true mountain climber can never give up as long as there is still an unconquered peak, so Paul could not let the Philippian believers give up until they had reached maturity. His challenge to them was to keep on walking, keep on growing, keep on climbing until they reached their potential in Christ.

David Jeremiah

GIFTS OF LIFE

It is more blessed to give than to receive.

ACTS 20:35

Too often we forget that it is a blessing to be able to give. If we were as eager to do things for others as we are to receive favors, we would better understand the words of Jesus, "It is more blessed to give than to receive." A spring of water continually gives, while a pool continually receives. That is why the spring is always fresh, while the pool becomes stagnant and filled with refuse. If we knew the blessing of giving, there would be no need for drives, schemes, rummage sales, car washes, entertainments, and circuses to support church work. The poor preacher would not need to plead and urge and beg to keep things going. A giving church cannot die, but when a people stop giving, the church dies—spiritually as well as materially.

After a minister had earnestly pleaded for the cause of missions, a stingy old deacon complained, "All this giving will kill the church." The pastor replied, "Take me to one church which died from giving and I will leap upon its grave and shout to high heaven, 'Blessed are the dead which die in the Lord!'"

EXPERIENCE PEACE

You have heard Me say to you, "I am going away and coming back to you." If you loved Me, you would rejoice because I said, "I am going to the Father."

JOHN 14:28

In order for Jesus to give us what He promised, it was necessary for Him to go back to heaven. He says in verse 28, "You have heard Me say to you, 'I am going away and coming back to you.' If you loved Me, you would rejoice because I said, 'I am going to the Father.'" Jesus is reminding His disciples (and us) that before His peace could flood their hearts, it was necessary for Him to ascend back to heaven and be with the Father.

You may wonder why that was true. I believe it was because the peace of the Lord Jesus is resident in the Person of the Holy Spirit, and the Holy Spirit could not be poured out upon humankind as He was at Pentecost until Jesus Christ ascended back to the Father. Jesus had just told the disciples (vv. 25–26) that the Holy Spirit would be sent by the Father after Jesus was no longer present with them. Because the Holy Spirit is resident in the life of every believer, it becomes possible for every believer to experience peace (Galatians 5:22).

David Jeremiah

HAPPY IS HE WHO OBEYS

Where there is no revelation, the people cast off restraint;
but happy is he who keeps the law.

PROVERBS 29:18

Roger Staubach, who led the Dallas Cowboys to the World Championship in 1971, admitted that it was difficult for him to be a quarterback who didn't call his own signals. Coach Tom Landry told Staubach when to pass, when to run, and only in emergency situations could he change the play. Even though Staubach considered Coach Landry to have a "genius mind" when it came to football strategy, pride told him he should have been able to run his own defense.

Staubach later said, "I faced up to the issue of obedience. Once I learned to obey, there was harmony, fulfillment, and victory."

Every Christian needs to come to terms with the issue of obedience as well. True happiness and fulfillment come in obeying God's commands. Many have turned down the wrong corridor in search of happiness. They have chased after possessions, pleasures, and positions, only to find themselves at a dead end. Disillusioned by a world that promised happiness, they stand before a chasm of emptiness and trouble.

Have you been searching for happiness in all the wrong places? True happiness awaits those who obey Christ.

THE MAN WITH A PLAN

He who has begun a good work in you will complete it until the day of Jesus Christ.

PHILIPPIANS 1:6

When a young teenage girl named Joni Eareckson broke her neck in a diving accident, she thought it was the last step on her road to life. In reality, her mishap was actually the first step on a path of fruitfulness that she could not have imagined at the time. From her wheelchair, the quadriplegic Joni Eareckson Tada has touched millions of lives through her books, art, music, and advocacy for the disabled.

Joni's story is more dramatic than anything most of us will ever experience. But the depth of her suffering serves all the more effectively to illustrate the point: the day we think life has come to an end is the day God's plans and purposes are brought into even sharper focus. What we call "accidents" in life are nothing of the sort if we mean that accidents are random occurrences outside of everyone's control—unpredictable events with no more meaning than a ricocheting steel ball in a pinball machine. The same God who has every hair on your head numbered has the days of your life numbered as well.

The child of God should rest in the knowledge that our Father in heaven has a plan—and He is never late.

David Jeremiah

TIMELESS REFUGE

Therefore we will not fear even though the earth be removed, and though the mountains be carried into the midst of the sea.

PSALM 46:2

We, as humans, are tied to time and space—they are all we know. We do not have a sense of the eternal. This earthly planet where we make our home is our point of reference in the universe. If it is stable, we feel secure. If it trembles and quakes, then we do as well. But God our refuge is not tied to this earth. In fact, He is not tied to anything. The entire earth could be removed, and the mountains could be carried into the midst of the sea; the waters could roar and be troubled, and the mountains could swell and shake—and God, our God, would still be a refuge.

The comfort for us in this is that nothing can happen to us in the time-and-space existence we live in that can impact God. He is, and will always be, a refuge for us. When things change around us, God doesn't change. When things are in an uproar around us, He is not. When things of the earth are in a calamitous state, He is at peace. Therefore He is always a timeless refuge where we can seek shelter and safety.

WE CAN DO IT!

The Lord is with us. Do not fear them.

NUMBERS 14:9

I love the story of the Israelites when they were in Kadesh Barnea (Numbers 13). Moses sent spies into the land to check it out. The majority came back and reported, "We can't do it. We checked it out, and we are like grasshoppers in front of the giants of the land." But Joshua and Caleb went to the same land, saw the same giants, and probably experienced the same initial fear, but they said, "We're no match for them, but they are no match for God. We can do it!" Joshua and Caleb were honored for their faith. That's why they got to go into the promised land while the other spies didn't.

When you worship God, when you praise Him, when you honor Him, when you hallow His name, your vision will be expanded. You will become a more visionary business-person, a more visionary spouse, a more visionary parent. You will see life not in the little restricted areas that are yours, but you will begin to see that part of your life expand into that which God wants to do through you.

David Jeremiah

SEE GOD AS HE REALLY IS

When He is revealed, we shall be like Him, for we shall see Him as He is.

1 JOHN 3:2

When you see God as He really is, you will worship Him as He desires to be worshiped. When Moses saw God and worshiped Him, he ended up giving us the law. When Job saw God and worshiped Him, his whole family was restored to him and he got his second start. When Isaiah saw the Lord high and lifted up, he was inducted into the role of a prophet. When Saul was struck by the holiness of God, he became Paul, the greatest missionary evangelist who ever lived. And when John saw God and fell down before him as dead, he got up and wrote the book of Revelation, the great apocalyptic story of the New Testament. Worship is not a noun; it's a verb. Worship is your whole life dedicated back to God.

Finally, when you see God as He really is, you will look forward to the day when you will be like Him. In the New Testament we are told that someday we shall be like Him because we will see Him as He is. On that day we will be holy in perfection. We will be changed and the sin of our lives will be taken away. We're going to be beautiful because God is beautiful in His holiness.

STRENGTHEN ONE ANOTHER

All things are lawful for me, but not all things are helpful; all things are lawful for me, but not all things edify. Let no one seek his own, but each one the other's well-being.

I CORINTHIANS 10:23–24

Y ou and I are called to build up and strengthen one another. I am called to build you up. You are called to build me up. I must be very careful not to tear you down by my actions, inaction, or words.

Tearing down is the polar opposite of our calling in Scripture. Edifying one another doesn't happen accidentally. Be on your knees before God, asking Him to fill you with His Spirit and show you opportunities. Be filled with the Word of God and begin to see people as individuals who need to be built up. Fight off the inevitable distractions and interruptions.

Paul is saying, "There are many things I might do and many things I might say. But my first concern ought to be, 'Will this build up or tear down my brother or sister in the body?'"

David Jeremiah

LOOK TO THE PAST

I remember the days of old, I meditate on all Your works;
I muse on the work of Your hands.

PSALM 143:5

One thing we can do as we stand at the threshold of transition is to remember how God has helped us in the past. Has He not been good to you? I know there has been some heartache, hurt, and tragedy in the last year. That's true for all of us, more true for some. As we survey all of what God has done, especially in perspective, God has been good to us. He has met our needs. As God has helped us in the past, He will help us in the future. I have witnessed how God has time and again helped our church. Sometimes we too have been at the Red Sea, the enemy has been right on our heels, the wall has been right in front of us, and at the last moment God has opened the way. That's the God we serve. God will lead us into the future. We have no need to fear since the God of the past is the God of the present.

THE GREATER WORKS

He who believes in Me, the works that I do he will do also; and greater works than these he will do, because I go to My Father.

JOHN 14:12

It is exciting to me to understand what begins to happen as we pray. It's not that we pray in order that *we* might do the work. Take another look at the verse: "And whatever you ask in My name, that will I do" (John 14:13). If you ask anything in His name, *He* will do it.

That is no small distinction! Sometimes Christians get weary because we forget. We think God wants us to do His work for Him. That will make you tired very, very quickly. You can't do it! I can't do it! Our legs are too short to run with God! What Jesus is saying is this: when we pray, God is going to do His work through us, and we will be channels for His work.

I remember hearing about a preacher who said he could build a great church even if there was no God. I'm not sure that's a compliment. Sometimes we do commendable, praiseworthy things in the energy of our flesh. But when God begins to do the work *through* us, it is an entirely different proposition altogether. Incredible things begin to happen.

David Jeremiah

OUR HOPE FOR NEW BODIES

The Lord Jesus Christ . . . will transform our lowly body that it may be conformed to His glorious body.

PHILIPPIANS 3:20–21

While we don't know exactly how our bodies are going to be changed in that glorious day, we do know that the limitations and pain and suffering and death will be forever gone! To the Corinthians, Paul said that our bodies will be buried in decay and raised without decay; they will be sown in humiliation and raised in splendor; they will be sown in weakness and raised in strength; they will be sown a physical body and raised a spiritual body (1 Corinthians 15).

Our new bodies will be like the glorious body of our Lord Jesus Christ. Apart from the resurrection of Jesus Himself, there are only three resurrections recorded in the Gospels: the son of the widow of Nain, the daughter of Jairus, and Lazarus. All of these situations began in mourning until Jesus came; then that sorrow was turned into joy and gladness. Jesus said of Himself, "I am the resurrection and the life" (John 11:25). Whenever the life of Jesus meets death, death is always defeated. When He comes again, death will be dealt its final blow. As Paul said to the Corinthians, "Death is swallowed up in victory" (15:54).

MAY

I will never leave you nor forsake you.

—HEBREWS 13:5

EVERY DAY WITH GOD

Every day I will bless you, and I will praise Your name forever and ever.

PSALM 145:2

A good way to think of eternity in the future is to think of it in terms of today. Has God provided for you and cared for you today? Not yesterday or tomorrow, but today? Wherever you are today, as you are reading this, has the Lord sustained you today?

Things aren't perfect, I realize. They never will be on earth. But regardless of today's imperfections, we can still confess that God has blessed us and is watching over us today.

Well, with God, every day is today. He is eternal. Do you think God is sitting up in heaven wringing His hands over what might happen to you tomorrow or the next day? God sees the end from the beginning. God lives in the eternal now. And if I am okay with God in the now, I have nothing to fear from the future, for every day with God is today, and He can be trusted.

David Jeremiah

GOD NEVER SLEEPS

Behold, He who keeps Israel shall neither slumber nor sleep.

PSALM 121:4

It is one of the most amazing facts about our God that He never slumbers or sleeps. What good is a God who is not there when you need Him? Elijah caught the idolatrous prophets of Baal on this very point in 1 Kings 18.

Elijah arranged a contest on the top of Mount Carmel to demonstrate to the prophets of Baal that the God of Israel was the only real and true God. They set up an altar with sacrifices on it, and whichever "god"—either Baal or Yahweh—could consume the sacrifices with fire from heaven would be the true God.

Just when the prophets needed Baal to prove his existence, he's taking a nap. Elijah seized the moment and called out to the true God, who sent down fire from heaven that licked up the sacrifices on the altar in a mighty display of His existence and His power. Think of yourself in your time of need on your journey through this life. Which "god" would you rather call upon to help you? The God of Israel neither slumbers nor sleeps. He is there at all hours of the day for you.

WHATEVER HE CHOOSES

For who in the heavens can be compared to the LORD? Who among the sons of the mighty can be likened to the LORD?

PSALM 89:6

A young boy was waiting after church for his family, and the pastor struck up a conversation with him. Since the boy had just come from Sunday school, the clergyman decided to ask a little question to see how much he was learning. He said, "Young man, if you can tell me something God can do, I'll give you this apple." The boy thoughtfully replied, "Sir, if you can tell me something God can't do, I'll give you a whole box of apples."

There really isn't anything God can't do. The Bible speaks of God's almighty power by using the word *omnipotent*. To be almighty is to have all the power. Only God has all the power. A theologian has defined the omnipotence of God like this: it is the power of God, or His ability and strength, whereby He can bring to pass whatsoever He pleases, whatsoever His infinite wisdom may direct, and whatsoever His purity of will may resolve. In other words, God is able to do whatever He chooses to do.

David Jeremiah

ANGELS REJOICE AT OUR SALVATION

Likewise, I say to you, there is joy in the presence of the angels of God over one sinner who repents.

LUKE 15:10

The Bible tells us that angels are aware of the moment each person repents of his sin and becomes a Christian. According to Luke 15:10, they rejoice. One writer says that "they set the bells of heaven to ringing with their rejoicing before the Lamb of God." Although the angels rejoice when people are saved and glorify God who has saved them, they cannot do one thing: they cannot testify personally to something they have not experienced. Angels have not been redeemed. They can only point to the experiences of the redeemed and rejoice that God has saved them. This means that throughout eternity, we humans alone will give our personal witness to the salvation that God achieved by grace and that we received through faith in Jesus Christ. As great as they are, angels cannot testify to salvation the same way as those who have experienced it.

VICTORY AND FRUITFUL LABOR

Therefore, my beloved brethren, be steadfast, immovable, always abounding in the work of the Lord, knowing that your labor is not in vain in the Lord.

1 CORINTHIANS 15:58

The greatest encouragement man will ever know is the giving of Jesus Christ to our world. Through His death, burial, and resurrection, Jesus has written the word *hope* in every heart. Because He lives, we too shall live. Because He was victorious over death, our future is bright.

As we consider the encouragement of Christ's resurrection, we should respond in two definite acts of love. Both of these responses are illustrated for each of us by the great apostle Paul. They are recorded in the last two verses of 1 Corinthians 15, the Bible's great resurrection chapter.

First, we should express our gratitude to our Father in heaven: "But thanks be to God, who gives us the victory through our Lord Jesus Christ" (1 Corinthians 15:57).

And second, we should do as Paul did—use the truth of Christ's resurrection to encourage others: "Therefore, my beloved brethren, be steadfast, immovable, always abounding in the work of the Lord, knowing that your labor is not in vain in the Lord" (1 Corinthians 15:58).

THE ADULTEROUS WOMAN

Neither do I condemn you; go and sin no more.

JOHN 8:11

Men have no right to judge others. No story better illustrates this than Jesus' encounter with the adulterous woman (John 8:3–11):

"As [Jesus] was speaking, the Jewish leaders and Pharisees brought a woman caught in adultery and placed her out in front of the staring crowd. 'Teacher,' they said to Jesus, 'this woman was caught in the very act of adultery. Moses' law says to kill her. What about it?' They were trying to trap him into saying something they could use against him, but Jesus stooped down and wrote in the dust with his finger.

They kept demanding an answer, so he stood up and said, 'All right, hurl the stones at her until she dies. But only he who never sinned may throw the first!' Then he stooped down again and wrote some more in the dust. And the Jewish leaders slipped away one by one, beginning with the eldest, until only Jesus was left in front of the crowd with the woman. Then Jesus stood up again and said to her, 'Where are your accusers? Didn't even one of them condemn you?' 'No sir,' she said. And Jesus said, 'Neither do I. Go and sin no more.'"

BE HUMBLE, BE WISE

When pride comes, then comes shame; but with the humble is wisdom.

PROVERBS 11:2

On December 6, 2001, American evangelist Billy Graham received a singular honor from the British Empire. He was given an honorary knighthood in recognition of his Christian service benefiting England and the world. When given his award by the British ambassador to the United States, the evangelist's remarks were characteristic: "I accept it with humility and unworthiness." He went on to say that he looked forward to laying his honorary knighthood, along with any other recognition he has ever received, at the feet of Jesus Christ, who deserves all the honor and praise.

One has to wonder if the impact of Billy Graham and his ministry around the world is in any way connected with his personal spirit of "humility and unworthiness." In light of biblical testimony concerning humility, the answer has to be yes. God gives skill and advancement to the humble and actively resists (stands in the way of) the proud. If you have a destination in view, you can remove at least one serious roadblock by being humble on the way.

Skills for living are not acquired as much as they are received in the form of grace—given by God as wisdom to the humble.

David Jeremiah

THE SPIRIT'S TRANSLATION

The Spirit helps us in our weakness. We do not know what we ought to pray for, but the Spirit himself intercedes for us with groans that words cannot express.

ROMANS 8:26 NIV

I heard a story about a pastor who frequently visited a woman who was dying from cancer. One day she told him, "I'm so often racked with pain that it's hard for me to gather my thoughts to pray. Even when I rally a little from the influence of the medication, my mind is still so dull I can't concentrate for any length of time."

He looked at her a moment and said, "Well, you can groan, can't you?"

"Oh yes," she replied, "My days are spent doing that."

"Well, never mind that you can't formulate prayers," the pastor told her. "The Holy Spirit translates your groans into eloquent petitions and presents them to the Father!"

Can you remember moments in your life when your heart was so heavy or your thoughts seemed so confused that you couldn't even find words to speak to God? Sometimes, even though we're on our knees in an attitude of prayer, we can only manage to sigh or groan or whisper the Lord's name. And in those moments, according to Paul, the indwelling Holy Spirit takes our sighs and our groans and brings those prayers to God. He understands the inward turmoil in our life. He is the searcher of our hearts, and He knows us better than we know ourselves.

WHEN GOD DELAYS

Can a woman forget her nursing child, and not have compassion on the son of her womb? Surely they may forget, yet I will never forget you.

ISAIAH 49:15

Let's be honest. Sometimes when God delays, we feel forgotten. Someone has said that it is the length of the trial, not the severity of it, done is most threatening to us. When a painful trial begins, we rally our resolve, we call our comrades, and we determine to defeat our "enemy." But as the days wear on and nothing changes, we lose heart and begin to grow weary. We never imagined God would let us suffer so long!

God says it is as likely that He would forget us as it is that a mother would forget her nursing child (Isaiah 49:15–16)—though it doesn't seem like it in the midst of our trials. Not only can we feel forgotten—we can feel forsaken as well.

So when you pray to God in your hour of seeming abandonment, just remember: God has heard that prayer before, even from His own Son. He knows what you are going through. In fact, He deliberately turned His back on His own Son so that He would never have to turn His back on us. He tells us, "I will never leave you nor forsake you."

David Jeremiah

HOW TO VALUE ANYTHING

He who tills his land will be satisfied with bread, but he who follows frivolity is devoid of understanding.

PROVERBS 12:11

Many men of the world have understood the necessity of commitment when trying to accomplish great things. Spanish explorer Cortez landed at Vera Cruz in 1519 to begin his conquest of Mexico with a small force of seven hundred men. It is said that when his entire crew came ashore, he purposely set fire to his fleet of eleven ships. Presumably, his men on the shore watched their only means of retreat sink to the bottom of the Gulf of Mexico. There was now only one direction to move—forward into the Mexican interior to meet whatever might come their way.

This illustration of diligence is a stark rebuke to those who believe that all of life's fruits can be had instantly and with little or no sacrifice. But in God's economy, the germination-cultivation-harvest cycle remains. And it is based on the application of diligence and commitment. Are you facing the temptation to give up on something important? What does your level of commitment say about the importance of the cause you have committed to?

The value we place on a relationship or project or opportunity can be measured directly by the degree of diligence we apply in working at it.

THE GOD OF ALL GRACE

The God of all grace . . . called you to His eternal glory in Christ.

1 PETER 5:10

God took Jacob through one experience after another to teach him to submit. Jacob even wrestled with God once, but his vow afterward rang hollow. Jacob didn't deserve any more chances, but God's grace stayed in effect. The Lord loved Jacob and disciplined him until he surrendered his life to God.

God is more forgiving than we can imagine. His continuing grace can take the sorry elements of a human life and use them for His blessed purposes. There is nothing more marvelous in the entire world than the power of God's grace. He forgives, He lifts up, and He transforms.

The great love of God's grace can heal broken hearts and mend broken lives. The gospel comes to hearts that are broken by sin and despairing of redemption, and it offers peace, pardon, and purity. Only a God of grace could take a rebellious man like Judah and a wicked woman like Tamar and somehow use them in the line of our Blessed Redeemer. But that's what God does—redeem people. He came to reclaim the broken lives of His children. He is the God of all grace, and His grace abounds to you and me.

ONE-ON-ONE CARE

Are not two sparrows sold for a copper coin? And not one of them falls to the ground apart from Your Father's will. . . . Do not fear, therefore; you are of more value than many sparrows.

MATTHEW 10:29, 31

God is the God of the individual. He is the God who would spare Sodom if someone there could demonstrate faith. When the destruction came, He got His people out because of His love for the individual. He was the one who saw Nathanael, sitting under a fig tree, and later talked to him one-on-one. He's the one who cared about Cornelius, who was praying by the sea. He's the one who sent two messengers to Rahab so that she could know what to do before the judgment came.

God knows who you are. He sees you in the massive crowd on this overpopulated globe! He knows you, He loves you, and He cares. The same God who is the God of patience is a God of passion for the individual.

He is the only one who can take us as we are and not only keep us from the judgment but also lift us up out of the mire and put our feet upon the Rock. He'll give us all we need to become all He ever wanted us to be.

ROOTED IN THE WORD OF GOD

His delight is in the law of the Lord. . . . He shall be like a tree planted by the rivers of water.

PSALM 1:2–3

Your strength comes from God's Word. The psalmist says the righteous person is like a tree planted by streams of water. Just like a tree is nourished by the constant supply of water—without which, under the blistering sun, the tree would surely die—so the life that is rooted in the Word of God will also be established and will be strong.

Your stability comes from God's Word. A fruit tree that is planted by the banks of the river suggests stability. The tree is firmly rooted in the soil so that it can resist the storm. There are trees standing today that were here when this country was discovered. If you go to the right place, you can see trees that are just as magnificent and beautiful as they were in their prime. Why? Because they've got a tremendous root structure and they are strong. If you've ever seen a redwood, a tree so big that you can drive your car through the middle of it, then you know what *invincible* means. That's the kind of stability God wants His people to have. And when you put your roots deep down into His Word, you will become a person of great stability.

David Jeremiah

JOY THAT STAYS

*I will see you again and your heart will rejoice, and your joy
no one will take from you.*

JOHN 16:22

The joy of Christ doesn't go away. Have you noticed how easily earthly joy can leave? Have you discovered how simple it is for your gladness of today to become your sadness of tomorrow, for your sweetness of the morning to turn into the bitterness of the night? Have you discovered how the people you thought were your friends today can become your enemies tomorrow, the wisdom you thought was so great yesterday is foolishness today?

Nothing seems to be too stable in the world. You can't really count on much anymore. But the joy of Christ is a continual, never-ending, absolutely constant joy when we follow the principles of the Word of God. This joy survives all the difficult times in life. This joy is not hinged on happenings but on a Person.

In John 16:22, Jesus says, "Therefore you now have sorrow; but I will see you again and your heart will rejoice, and your joy no one will take from you." Isn't that something? Jesus says the joy He wants to give every one of His children is the kind of joy you don't have to lose. Nobody can take it away from you!

WHEN GOD SEEMS UNFAIR

You say, "The way of the Lord is not fair." Hear now . . . is it not My way which is fair, and your ways which are not fair?"

EZEKIEL 18:25

That's not fair! Did you ever say that to your parents? Most of us have, and in some cases we have spoken the truth. But usually children feel that way because they're unable to see things from a more mature perspective.

In Isaiah 55:8–9, our heavenly Father says: "My thoughts are not your thoughts, nor are your ways My ways. . . . For as the heavens are higher than the earth, so are My ways higher than your ways, and My thoughts than your thoughts."

Abraham might have wondered if God was being too harsh with the population of Sodom, but he contented himself with this assurance: "Shall not the Judge of all the earth do right?" (Genesis 18:25).

He shall! God is righteous—that is, He is morally right, and He is right in His decisions and in all His ways. But God tempers His justice with mercy. If you sometimes feel God has treated you unfairly, tell Him so. Then ask Him to give you a higher understanding of His ways and a deeper dependence on His grace. You can trust the Judge of all the earth to do right.

David Jeremiah

THE INDESTRUCTIBLE WORD

The grass withers, the flower fades, but the Word of our God stands forever.
ISAIAH 40:8

Down through the centuries, the Bible has always been hated and scorned by God's enemies. Men have gone out of their way to abolish it.

There have been some "heroes" of God's Word. William Tyndale devoted his life to spreading God's good news. He translated it, printed it, and distributed it. In the midst of the great distribution under Tyndale, the bishop got angry and wanted to get the Bibles out of circulation. He sent a friend to buy all the Bibles Tyndale had printed. "Whatever it takes, buy them and destroy them." The friend talked Tyndale out of the Bibles in spite of Tyndale's exorbitant price. The bishop's friend paid it, took the Bibles, and destroyed them. With the money from the Bibles, Tyndale bought materials to print thirty times as many Bibles and distributed them all over the country. When the bishop discovered more Bibles, he asked where Tyndale had gotten the funds to do this. His friend said, "You paid for it—you bought the Bibles and he distributed them."

Isn't that great! The Bible, defiantly, victoriously, convincingly, still stands. It remains the only inerrant, infallible, complete revelation man has ever received from his living God.

DOING THE STEPS

The fear of the Lord is the beginning of wisdom, and the knowledge of the Holy One is understanding.

PROVERBS 9:10

A little boy comes to his father: "Daddy, I can't get this piece of my model car to fit. I know it goes right there, but there's just not room." After walking his son back through the directions, they discover together that the problem part should have been glued in on step four—and the little guy is nearly finished. "See what happens? They tell you to put this piece in early because they know there won't be room once the others are assembled."

Sometimes when life's pieces don't fit together, it may be because we skipped the first step. And the first step to gaining wisdom and God's knowledge is to fear the Lord. The word *beginning* can mean either "the first part" or "the main part." In both cases, the practical message is the same. The first step, and the continual priority, in fitting all the part of life together is to honor, revere, and worship God. Why? Because all knowledge and wisdom come from God, and we must seek answers through Him if we are to find them at all.

If you're stumped with a part of life that won't fit, humble yourself before the Lord. That's the first step in living life skillfully.

David Jeremiah

PROBLEMS PREPARE US FOR MINISTRY

[God] comforts us in all our tribulation, that we may be able to comfort those who are in any trouble, with the comfort with which we ourselves are comforted by God.

2 CORINTHIANS 1:4

Problems in our lives make us sensitive to the problems of others. How could the men and women of God reach out to a hurting world if they had never experienced that same pain in their own lives? How can we put our arms around a brother facing disappointment if we have never experienced disappointment ourselves? Sometimes God allows problems in our lives so that we can better minister to someone else. That's exactly what happened to Joseph. From his humbling slave and prison experiences, he was able to fairly administer grain to a starving populace.

You see, problems have advantages. They provide us with opportunities if we will but look for them. They promote spiritual maturity if we let them make us better instead of bitter. They prove our integrity, produce a sense of dependency, and prepare our hearts for ministry. God allows problems so that we can learn and grow. We don't like them, but they are necessary if we are to grow and change. Don't run from the pressures God wants to use to make you His perfect example of Christlikeness.

FEEDING SHEEP

Jesus said to [Peter], "Feed My sheep."

JOHN 21:17

The final chapter of John's gospel records one of the last conversations between the resurrected Lord Jesus and Peter. Just days earlier, Peter had denied his Lord beside a fire. Now, beside another fire, he will be restored. Just as Peter had denied Christ three times, he would be given three opportunities to confess his love for Jesus.

That's the portion of the story most people remember. Jesus uses one word for love—a strong, intense word for committed love—and Peter, his confidence shattered, comes back with a weaker word in reply. That happens two times, until finally Jesus looks Peter in the eyes and uses Peter's own, weaker word, as if to say, "Peter, do you even care for Me as a friend?"

The question breaks the big fisherman's heart, but Jesus neither rejects nor casts the sorrowing man aside. On the contrary, He sends Peter into the kingdom. In no uncertain terms, He gives him a job to do.

That is the portion of the story so often overlooked. Every time Peter answered the Lord, the Lord gave him a strong, specific command: "Feed my lambs, Peter"; "Tend my sheep, Peter"; "Feed my sheep, Peter."

Peter got the message. Do you?

David Jeremiah

UNWILLING HOPE

This hope we have as an anchor of the soul, both sure and steadfast.

HEBREWS 6:19

Scripture teaches us that hope is necessary because the will is often uncooperative. We all know we should possess hope. We know that as Christians, we should be filled with hope. But how many of us have found ourselves praying the prayer of Paul in Romans 7:19: "Lord, I know what I should do, but I don't do it. I know what I shouldn't do, and here I am doing it again" (my paraphrase).

Hebrews 6:18 is very interesting. It says, "That by two immutable things, in which it is impossible for God to lie, we might have strong consolation, who have fled for refuge to lay hold of the hope set before us."

Many of us have experienced difficult times and we know our hope ought to be in the Lord. But sometimes our will is uncooperative and we just have to forget everything, hang on to God, and flee to Him for our refuge

THE SPIRIT'S GIFTS

To each one of us grace was given according to the measure of Christ's gift.

EPHESIANS 4:7

The Bible says that when you're saved you not only get the Giver, you get the gift! You receive the Spirit of God, but you also receive the gift of the Spirit. Every Christian is immediately endowed with a special gift of ministry. You will find those gifts listed in Romans 12, in Ephesians 4, and in 1 Corinthians 12.

In other words, every believer has a gift of the Spirit. We are to exercise that gift so that everyone else profits. I exercise my gift, and it helps you. You exercise your gift, and it helps me. And all of us using our giftedness help the whole body to grow. But you can't do that without the Spirit of God. The whole concept of service is based on the spiritual filling of the believer. No wonder so many of God's people are trying to figure out how to survive! Do you know what we're trying to do? We're trying to accomplish a supernatural task in the energy of our own weak flesh.

We run like crazy trying to keep up with everything, and we fall into bed at night totally exhausted. There is no human way for us to do the work of God in the energy of the flesh. If the Spirit of God doesn't fill us with His power, we're attempting the impossible.

David Jeremiah

NINETY-TWO BANANAS

God shall supply all your need according to His riches in glory by Christ Jesus.
PHILIPPIANS 4:19

The prophet Jeremiah and the apostle Paul discovered the same thing about prayer: when our hearts are right, God delights to give us more than we asked for. In Jeremiah 33:3, the Lord said, "Call to Me, and I will answer you, and show you great and mighty things, which you do not know." In Ephesians 3:20, Paul said that God "is able to do exceedingly abundantly above all that we ask or think."

In her autobiography, *Evidence Not Seen*, missionary Darlene Diebler tells of being near starvation in a Japanese POW camp. Through her window she saw in the distance a banana. "Lord," she prayed, "just one banana." But she couldn't see how God could get her a banana through prison walls.

The next day she heard footsteps coming down the hall and the key turning in the door of her cell. In walked a guard with a bunch of bananas. "They're yours," he said. She sat down in stunned silence and counted them. There were ninety-two bananas!

As Darlene wept and thanked the Lord, she seemed to hear Him say in her heart, "That's what I delight to do, exceeding abundantly above everything you ask or think."

A REFLECTION OF HOLINESS

I will make all My goodness pass before you, and I will proclaim the name of the Lord before you.

EXODUS 33:19

What happened to Moses when he experienced the Holy? Moses had seen some pretty amazing miracles in his life, but he still wanted to see God's glory. God decided to show Moses a little bit of His glory. God put Moses in the cleft of a rock and covered him with His hand as He passed by. Moses saw only a reflection of the holiness of God from a distant rear view, but it affected him so much that the people of Israel were afraid of him when they saw him. His face shone so brilliantly that the people were terrified. Moses had to wear a veil in order to talk to the people.

If we could see God as He really is, not only would we know Him as a God of compassionate love, but we would see Him as a God of holiness, quite apart from anything we have ever known.

Why is it important to see God as He really is in His holiness? Because only then will you see yourself as you really are.

David Jeremiah

A FAMILY FOCUSED ON GOD

*And Joseph situated his father and his brothers, and gave them possession
in the land of Egypt, in the best of the land, in the land of Ramses,
as Pharaoh had commanded.*

GENESIS 47:11

There are at least three lessons we can learn from the story of Joseph and his family. First, God provided for the entire family due to the faithfulness of one member. God provided good land, met their every need, and watched Jacob's family come back to Him, and none of it would have happened had it not been for Joseph. Christians, if we are the only godly people in our families, we can't quit. We have the potential of redeeming our entire family.

A second lesson we learn from this story is that we are to care for the elderly. Joseph sets an example for us to follow by offering tender, loving care to his father.

Finally, we learn that God puts a priority on the family. The family is part of God's perfect plan for the world. There are only two institutions that God ordained: the church and the family. In this day, when families are being torn apart, the story of Joseph is a clear indication of what the family can accomplish when it is intact and focused on the Lord.

NO COOKIE-CUTTER CHILDREN

The father of the righteous will greatly rejoice, and he who begets a wise child will delight in him.

PROVERBS 23:24

Sometimes we have the parenting cookie-cutter mentality. We not only want our children to believe what we believe, but we want them to live out their beliefs exactly like we do. We lose sight of the fact that as children grow, they are going to develop some of their own ways of expressing the same commitments to truth that we have. But when we lose sight of the commitment to truth and we demand outward conformity in every single way, we foster rebellion, because rebellion is the only way they can get enough energy and power to be what they need to be.

You may have heard the story about the housewife who always cut off the end of a ham before baking it in her oven. When the reason was discovered, it was because her grandmother's small oven necessitated it—a practice that was blindly followed by succeeding generations without question. Values and beliefs should not change from generation to generation, but the expression of them likely will. When we force our children to express their beliefs as we do, we foster rebellion. They need freedom to become their own people.

David Jeremiah

MEEKNESS, NOT WEAKNESS

Blessed are the meek, for they shall inherit the earth.

MATTHEW 5:5

When you hear the word *meekness,* you may think of the word in its modern setting—someone who is spineless, spiritless, lacking in strength and virility. The meek person in today's world is not how we'd like to be known.

But the Bible says, "Blessed are the meek." The Bible says the meek are blessed of God and someday they will rule the earth.

Meekness is not weakness. It is not laziness. It is not compromise at any price, not just being born nicer than other people.

The word came to mean in classical Greek "to soothe, to calm, to tranquilize." Someone has described meekness as gentleness by those who have the power to be otherwise—power under control. Meekness is the grace that brings strength and gentleness together.

When Jesus invited us to Him, He did not appeal to us on the basis of His kingship, majesty, or authority. The Lord reaches out His arms and says, "Come to Me and I'll give you rest, for I am meek—you can be comfortable coming to Me" (see Matthew 11:28).

THE SPIRIT'S PRESENCE

Do you not know that your body is the temple of the Holy Spirit who is in you, whom you have from God?

1 CORINTHIANS 6:19

Paul said to the Corinthians, "Do you not know that your body is the temple of the Holy Spirit?" Why was he telling them that? Because the Corinthians were doing things with their bodies that were an embarrassment to the Holy Spirit. They were living lives divorced from the awareness of His holy presence within them.

Perhaps you've found yourselves at certain crossroads recently where you didn't know whether you should go to a certain place or participate in a certain activity because you are a Christian. The fact is, where you go, the Holy Spirit goes with you. So before you go, you'd better ask Him if *He* wants to go. And whatever He tells you, do it.

Many Christians don't even think about that. They just drag the Holy Spirit everywhere, into all kinds of things that are dishonoring to His first name, which is *Holy*.

The Holy Spirit permanently indwells you. If you grasp that concept, it could have a life-changing impact on you. He is there. He is in you. He will never leave you.

David Jeremiah

ABUNDANTLY GOOD

Great is the L<small>ORD</small>, and greatly to be praised; and His greatness is unsearchable.
P<small>SALM</small> 145:3

When the Bible writers call God good, they are thinking of all those things about His character we admire: His perfection, His compassion, His mercy, His grace, and perhaps most of all, His generosity.

Whatever God is, He is abundantly! God is good in a generous way. That means God loves to lavish upon His children that which blesses them. God is blessed in His life when He brings joy and blessing to those who depend upon Him for sustaining grace. Just as we have a real sense of joy in our hearts when we are able to do something good for another person, God has an intense joy in His heart as He expresses His goodness to all of us.

Have you ever heard a sermon about the prodigal son where the father is described as prodigal? *Prodigal* means "lavish, unrestrained, and unlimited." If you want to see the prodigal in that story, examine the heart of the father who never stopped loving his wayward son. Who waited every day to see him come home. And who, when his wayward son walked back into the family home, put on a feast to welcome him back. There was nothing that father would not do for his son. That's the way God is. He lavishes Himself upon His people.

THE SOVEREIGNTY OF GOD

God sent me before you to preserve a posterity for you in the earth, and to save your lives by a great deliverance. So now it was not you who sent me here, but God.
GENESIS 45:7–8

I've noticed, as I've studied the life of Joseph, that God is just as intimate to him as breath. God is so much a part of Joseph's life that he sees the Lord in every circumstance, and he trusts the Lord through every difficulty. "God meant it for good," he tells his brothers, "in order to bring it about as it is this day, to save many people alive." Everything that happened to him, both bad and good, was viewed through the lens of God's will.

When Joseph interpreted Pharaoh's dream, he said that it was God who gave him the meaning. When Joseph presented his sons to Jacob, he introduced them by saying, "These are the two sons God has given me." Even when Joseph was dying, he was able to encourage those around him that "God will surely visit you."

At the center of Joseph's life was the sovereignty of God. Everything that happened was for His purposes and part of His program. Even the darkest threads in the weave help to provide the overall beauty of the tapestry.

David Jeremiah

SINGLE PEACE

He who is unmarried cares for the things of the Lord—how he may please the Lord.

1 CORINTHIANS 7:32

People are single for four kinds of reasons: physical, medical, spiritual, or they just want to be single (not everybody wants to be married and apparently that is a part of God's plan). Some of the greatest people who ever served God were single. Rejoice in all the gifts God has given you, including your singleness.

Seeking marriage is not wrong, but don't let that search dominate your life. We must not make finding a marriage partner the supreme goal of our lives by putting all our energies into searching for a mate. We must learn to be in God's will. A very wise person said, "There is something far worse than single loneliness, and that is marital misery." Learn contentment, for it is great gain.

If God has a mate for you, He knows how to bring the two of you together. Don't take things into your own hands.

Wherever you are, whatever your situation, use the time to grow both mentally and spiritually.

DON'T ASK, DO

According to all that God commanded [Noah], so he did.

GENESIS 6:22

Noah did "according to all that God commanded" (Genesis 6:22). Therein lies the key and secret to Noah's faith. When God told him to do something, he did it. He was a man who took God at His word. We have no record of Noah disagreeing with God or debating His instructions. He believed that his salvation depended on God's wisdom and good plan, and he chose to receive it and implement it just as God explained it.

For us to be saved and move ahead as men and women of faith, we have to do the same thing. God needs to know that we are not going to debate or disagree with Him. His Word to us becomes our command. You and I will likely never be in Noah's position—the only person on earth who will obey God. But we need to live like it anyway. If we do, God will remember us the same way He remembered His friend Noah (Genesis 8:1).

JUNE

God is my strength and power,
and He makes my way perfect.

—2 SAMUEL 22:33

COME TO KNOW HIM

I know whom I have believed and am persuaded that He is able to keep what I have committed to Him until that Day.

2 TIMOTHY 1:12

We worship whom we trust, and we trust whom we know. We come to this level of faith because we build trust, and we build trust because we spend time with God. Do you remember the experience of getting to know your best friend—perhaps the person you married? You didn't fully unburden your deepest thoughts because you didn't know whether you could trust your new friend. Alas, there are lesser relationships with people who fall by the wayside because they betray our trust in some way. But your best friend was that person who redeemed your trust, and you confirmed it only through the time and tears of relationship.

The same principle holds true with God. You must come to know Him before you can really, truly, deeply trust Him. Then and only then will you be able to worship in spirit and in trust. Then and only then will you be able to say, in a twenty-first century paraphrase of Habakkuk, "I may lose my work, my loved ones, and all that I own. Still I will love God all the more. Still I will praise Him with the loudest voice I can muster. And He will lift me up, for I know whom I have believed and am persuaded that He is able."

David Jeremiah

THE POWER OF LIVING WATER

"He who believes in Me, as the Scripture has said, out of his heart will flow rivers of living water." But this He spoke concerning the Spirit.
JOHN 7:38–39

The greatest danger to any ancient city during a time of siege was not the enemy without; it was the lack of resources within. More often than not, when an army like the Assyrians attacked a walled city like Jerusalem, they would simply surround the city and wait for it to run out of food and water. Then, when the people were weak and desperate, the city could be taken almost without a fight. But Hezekiah made sure that would not happen to Jerusalem. He rerouted a spring of water outside the city walls so it flowed inside the walls of the city.

Interestingly, Jesus referred often to the Holy Spirit as the living water given by God to the believer, that constitutes a secret, powerful resource in times of trouble. When you have the Holy Spirit living inside of you, you possess a resource that can give you abundant life through the longest siege of the enemy. The enemy can camp at your doorstep for an indefinite period of time, and it won't matter to you. The Holy Spirit is your indwelling source of life.

PUT GOD FIRST

To You I have cried out, O LORD, and in the morning my prayer comes before You.
PSALM 88:13

I remember reading about a great prayer warrior, Andrew Murray, who said that sometimes he had so much to do that he had to add an extra hour to his prayers. As a flawed human being, I have often rushed through my day trying to accomplish my work without taking time to pray. Those are the times I get to the end of the day fatigued, frustrated, and with a sense of failure.

But if I push my work aside and refuse to tackle it until I have met with God, my work is energized. I don't know how it happens, but it does. More things happen in less time. Better things happen that would not happen otherwise. I'm not a mystic, nor am I trying to read something into this that isn't there. I'm just saying that when you put God first, God takes care of you. He takes care of the things you need.

David Jeremiah

NEVER TIRED

Have you not known? Have you not heard? The everlasting God, the LORD, the Creator of the ends of the earth, neither faints nor is weary.

ISAIAH 40:28

Everything that you and I do takes energy from us and causes our energy level to reduce. While there are some people who seem to have unlimited energy, nobody really does.

The older we get, the more we realize we can't do some of the things we did when we were younger. But the power of God is never diminished. When He exercises His great power on behalf of anyone or anything, all of His power is still at the same level. He is never tired.

Isaiah said, "Have you not known? Have you not heard? The everlasting God, the Lord, the Creator of the ends of the earth, neither faints nor is weary" (Isaiah 40:28). You don't need to wait and give God a chance to rest up. You can go to God at any time and know that all of His power is available to you.

GOD WORKS ALL THINGS
FOR GOOD

And we know that all things work together for good to those who love God, to those who are the called according to His purpose.

ROMANS 8:28

When President Roosevelt was in office, a madman once took a shot at him, wounding the president in the arm. A steel glasses case, which the president kept in his breast pocket, deflected the bullet and saved his life. The funny thing is, President Roosevelt hated that glasses case. It was heavy and burdensome, and he had often complained about it. But in the process of God's providence, the thing he hated saved his life.

Joseph's is a similar story. Though at times Joseph may have hated his situation and wondered about God's purposes, eventually his life was an example of the rule of God's providence. God took the darkest events and used them as stepping stones to move Joseph into position. Even when Joseph couldn't understand what God was doing, the Lord was still at work. God had been arranging the situation, even when it seemed like He was far away. In the end, Joseph realized God had worked all things out for good.

Joseph had it all in perspective. He saw that God was using even the evil things of this world to illustrate His providential work in the lives of men.

David Jeremiah

MEMORIALS OF GOD'S FAITHFULNESS

This is My name forever; and this is My memorial to all generations.

EXODUS 3:15

God wants us to have memorials so we won't forget. He preserved Noah and his family through the flood and then gave them the memorial of the rainbow. From that day on, we can look into the sky at a rainbow and remember how God delivered Noah and has promised never again to destroy the earth by water.

God gave the Israelites the ark of the covenant that they carried with them. Inside the ark were the Law that God had given to Moses on Mt. Sinai, the stone tablets to remember when God had given His people a code of conduct by which to live, and a little jar. The Bible says that inside that jar was some of the manna God had fed the people during their forty years of wandering. Why manna? It was another memorial to the fact that God can feed people right there in the desert where there were no restaurants.

The Lord was wise. He instituted memorials. Why? Because we have a tendency to forget. We need to remember that we have a God who has worked in the past, and because He has worked in the past, He is willing to work in the present.

GOD'S BEAUTY TREATMENT

Charm is deceitful and beauty is passing, but a woman who fears the LORD, she shall be praised.

PROVERBS 31:30

Americans spend billions of dollars every year on cosmetics, but the best beauty treatment isn't found in a bottle, but in a book—the Bible. First Peter 3:3–5 says, "Do not let your adornment be merely outward—arranging the hair, wearing gold, or putting on fine apparel—rather let it be the hidden person of the heart, with the incorruptible beauty of a gentle and quiet spirit, which is very precious in the sight of God. For in this manner, in former times, the holy women who trusted in God also adorned themselves."

Little is said of the physical qualities of the woman in Proverbs 31, though we assume she had a pleasant appearance. It is her character that's emphasized—her trustworthiness (v. 11), her hard work (v. 13), her business instincts (v. 16), her generosity (v. 20), her creativity (v. 22), her initiative (v. 24), and her strength (v. 25).

It's not the makeup on her face but the makeup of her heart that makes her beautiful. We can't all be fashion models, but we can all be fashioned by grace as models of our Lord Jesus Christ.

David Jeremiah

THE DANGER OF PROCRASTINATION

Blessed are those servants whom the master, when he comes, will find watching.

LUKE 12:37

Jesus tells a story of two slaves who work for an absentee master. One slave is good and faithful, and the other is evil and faithless. The good slave represents believers who will be on the earth before the Lord's return, while the evil servant represents unbelievers. Every person in the world holds his life, his possessions, and his abilities in trust from God, and they will all be held accountable to the Lord for what they have done with that trust. In the case of this evil servant, the dominant attitude is one of calloused procrastination. He doesn't believe the master is going to come back anytime soon, so he has no motivation to cease doing evil. Christ's words warn him to be careful because he doesn't know the schedule.

A man told me not long ago that he wanted to become a Christian, but it wasn't convenient for him right now. Well, because it wasn't convenient for that man to accept Christ, it won't be convenient for him to get into heaven.

There is going to be a day when that decision has to be made or it will no longer be available. If you haven't trusted Him yet, why don't you do it today? Receive Him as your Savior and your Lord.

A PARENT'S IMPACT

And he arose and came to his father. But when he was still a great way off, his father saw him and had compassion, and ran and fell on his neck and kissed him.

LUKE 15:20

One writer I read said that the way parents treat their children in daily living has more impact on their children's spiritual development than the family's religious practices, including having a family altar, reading the Bible together, and attending church services regularly.

Parenting is a difficult job. But we need to remember that when the rebellious son in Luke 15 came to himself, he found a loving father waiting for him at home. That father had probably made mistakes in his parenting, but he did not stop loving either of his two sons—and the younger son, at least, knew it.

Sometimes the stress of parenting makes us want to stop loving and leave. But if we remain and continue to love, we do more to negate the chances of rebellion in our children than anything we could ever do. May God help us to love our children as He loves us.

David Jeremiah

LIKE RIDING A BIKE

Blessed are all those who put their trust in Him.

PSALM 2:12

Do you remember learning to ride a bicycle? It was a trust issue—nothing more, nothing less. There came a time when you had to take the training wheels off, place your feet on the pedals, and allow that bike to take flight down the street.

No textbook, no parental word of advice would accomplish the mission. But once you made the leap of faith, you never again lost the aptitude for bike riding. Why? *Trust*.

To experience the fullness of worship, we must trust the One we worship. And to trust Him, we must know Him. Have you ever felt as if you knew all the facts about God but your prayers never passed the ceiling? Have you ever sung a hymn without being able to bring the words to life? Have you ever realized that your morning devotions have become a dry Bible study rather than a warm visit with your heavenly Father?

We need truth, and we need sound theology. The right information is essential. But above all else, we need *relationship*. Once we've come into His powerful and loving presence, we'll never struggle to trust Him again any more than we'll have to take a refresher course in bike riding.

THE COMPASSION OF GOD

By You I have been upheld from birth; You are He who took me out of my mother's womb.

PSALM 71:6

We have the theology for prosperity down pat, but sooner or later our prosperity will give way to adversity. If you don't have your theology finely tuned for that part of your life, you won't do well. Unexpected, unannounced, uncharted, unplanned—adversity comes to everyone.

Every believer should be able to review the compassion of God. Stop and think about all the paths God has led you down like a shepherd throughout your spiritual life. God has been faithful to you! Is there any reason you have to doubt His faithfulness now? As the psalmist says, from our mother's womb God took us, and He has upheld us from our birth.

Even if we have been a believer for only a matter of days or weeks, the grace of God has brought us life and health and strength. God's past faithfulness and compassion toward us is a heritage upon which we build our faith in the future.

David Jeremiah

PLUG IN TO HIS POWER

God is my strength and power, and He makes my way perfect.

2 SAMUEL 22:33

I have little power, but God has all power. If it is going to be, it is going to be up to Him. He has the power not only to bring things into existence, but to keep them out of existence as well. I have conceived a lot of things in my mind that God, in His wisdom and by His grace, has kept me from having. He has the power to do both.

So every day I need to end my prayer saying, "Lord, I know that, first of all, You are in control. Thank You. My life may seem out of control, but You are not. You are in control." The throne in heaven is not empty. God is there, seated and in sovereign control. He said a word and the worlds were made. He spoke and the moon and stars were flung out into space. He's an awesome, almighty, powerful God.

And my prayer links me with Him. I don't have to get up every morning and psych myself up for the day, because God's power is always there. All I've got to do is plug in to Him.

DILIGENT IN ALL THINGS

The desire of the lazy man kills him, for his hands refuse to labor.

PROVERBS 21:25

Billy Graham tells this of his upbringing: "I was taught that laziness was one of the worst evils, and there was dignity and honor in labor. I could abandon myself enthusiastically to milking the cows, cleaning out the latrines, and shoveling manure, not because they were pleasant jobs, but because sweaty labor held its own satisfaction."

Through godly rearing, Billy Graham developed the valuable character quality of diligence. A diligent man is one who works hard at every task, no matter how important or how menial. He uses his time efficiently and always puts forth his best work. Though he may feel sluggish at times, he refuses to be a sluggard. He is a man ruled by discipline, not feelings.

Against the backdrop of people who avoid work, cut corners, and do halfhearted jobs, a diligent man stands out. Practicing diligence is an excellent way to stand out for Christ at home, in the workplace, and even at church. Today, complete each one of your tasks, however big or small, with diligence.

David Jeremiah

STILL WATERS

In quietness and confidence shall be your strength.

ISAIAH 30:15

Have you ever felt like a goldfish swimming around in a blender full of water—with someone's finger on the "high" switch? Many of us are altogether too busy, running on overdrive, overextended in our schedules and under-developed in our souls. Instead of green pastures and still waters, we're accustomed to clogged freeways and blaring cell phones.

King Solomon is a good example of a man who was so busy in the work of God that he neglected his walk with God. The result? He developed a great empire and a lean soul. The Lord is more concerned with our relationship with Him than with our productivity for Him, and the wise person knows that a healthy soul requires a certain amount of "quiet" and "still" and "rest."

"Come aside by yourselves to a deserted place and rest a while," Jesus told the disciples in Mark 6:31. "Be still and know that I am God," advises the Lord in Psalm 46:10.

Is something in your life consuming you, pulling you away from intimacy with God? Are you too busy for your own good? A man had a plaque installed on his dashboard that read "Beware the Barrenness of Busyness." Why not take a deep breath, get away from all distractions, open your Bible, and commune with Him right now?

GOD'S ROAD MAP

I have led you forty years in the wilderness. Your clothes have not worn out on you, and your sandals have not worn out on your feet.

DEUTERONOMY 29:5

If we are honest, most of us will admit that we can deal with things that have a precedent, but walking into uncharted territory provokes fear. It is awesome to consider the thoughts that can fill our minds as we look into a future for which we have no road map. There were some things that God used to strengthen His people, and these things are available to us today as we face our challenges as well.

The people of Israel, standing on the bank of the Jordan River, had one sure thing. They had the record of God's performance on their behalf in the past.

For forty years, God's people had been wandering in the desert, yet God wonderfully and miraculously cared for them. First, they got into the wilderness through the miracle of walking through the Red Sea, and then God gave them a guidance system. Each day, for forty years, they were led by a pillar of cloud. At night they were led by a pillar of fire. They were wandering, but God was leading them. God spoke through Moses, "I have led you forty years in the wilderness. Your clothes have not worn out on you, and your sandals have not worn out on your feet."

David Jeremiah

JOY DOES NOT DEPEND ON CIRCUMSTANCES

Finally, my brethren, rejoice in the Lord.

PHILIPPIANS 3:1

Happiness is the world's cheap imitation of Christian joy. Happiness is dependent on happenings, on "hap," which is another word for "luck." Someone who is hapless is luckless.

When we have "joy," it can be our constant possession because it does not depend on the circumstances of the day. Paul said, "Rejoice in the Lord!" This philosophy made it possible for him to endure all kinds of problems and still move forward in his walk with Christ. When he wrote his second letter to the church at Corinth, he listed just a few of the things he had endured. Now we know how he endured them. He had the strength of genuine joy in his life.

How could any one man experience all these things and still have the spirit of joy? Paul understood what most modern men do not—that joy and pain are often compatible emotions.

THE GIFT OF FAME

He Himself gave some to be apostles, some prophets, some evangelists, and some pastors and teachers, for the equipping of the saints for the work of ministry.

EPHESIANS 4:11—12

To many people, fame is nearly as desirable as wealth. This is because acceptance is one of our basic needs, and there's nothing like seeing your name in bright lights to make you feel accepted and admired. Some come to fame because of exceptional talent or brilliance. Others just happen upon it, being at the right place at the right time. Artist Andy Warhol once predicted that, due to expanding TV technology, we'll all experience fame at some point in our lives, even if for just ten or fifteen minutes. Fame is fleeting, as they say, but elusiveness only adds to its enticement.

Christians should avoid the allure of fame. It can seduce us away from our foremost desire to serve God. Paul tells us that the Holy Spirit gives us gifts. We are to discover our gifts and be diligent with them, using them for God's glory. Because of the nature of certain gifts, some of their beneficiaries may incidentally become famous. But the real purpose of spiritual gifts is to lead the church to a more meaningful relationship with the Lord.

David Jeremiah

SATAN IS DOOMED

*The weapons of our warfare are not carnal but mighty in God
for pulling down strongholds.*

2 CORINTHIANS 10:4

The ultimate victory has been won at Calvary, but it will be implemented in the future. The sentence has been passed; now it needs to be enforced. The enforcement is in the hands of the church. The tool that enforces Satan's defeat is the tool of prayer. "For the weapons of our warfare are not carnal but mighty in God for pulling down strongholds, casting down arguments and every high thing that exalts itself against the knowledge of God, bringing every thought into captivity to the obedience of Christ" (2 Corinthians 10:4–5). One person praying on earth can move angels in heaven.

Christians need to learn the power of prayer against Satan, for he will be defeated in his work. We are not engaged in the warfare if we are not praying against Satan. The judgment that was effected at the cross and is enforced through prayer will be completed. Satan is doomed. Satan is on a leash, and he is only free on earth to the length of his chain. He cannot go beyond God's permission. But if we don't enforce his judgment in our own lives, we will be victims instead of victors.

THE SPIRIT'S WITNESS

The Spirit Himself bears witness with our spirit that we are children of God.
ROMANS 8:16

In Romans 8:16, Paul told the Romans, "The Spirit Himself bears witness with our spirit that we are children of God."

Wherever I travel across this country, people ask me, "How can I have assurance of salvation? How can I know that I really belong to Christ?" There are many scriptures to which we can point, but the bottom line is this: if you have the Holy Spirit living within you, that Spirit testifies with your spirit that you are a child of God. It is the inward witness of your faith.

Most of us have had the experience of saying to people, "I don't know exactly how to explain it, but I *know* I'm a Christian."

"Well, how do you know?"

"I just know inside."

We know inside because the Spirit of God is there, witnessing to our assurance. Somewhere within us, a voice whispers, *You are Mine. You are not your own. You belong to Me.*

David Jeremiah

A SACRIFICE OF PRAISE

By Him let us continually offer the sacrifice of praise to God, that is, the fruit of our lips, giving thanks to His name.

HEBREWS 13:15

In the month that lies before you, you'll have countless opportunities for sacrifice. Think of that person at work whom you struggle to love. What if you visualize yourself placing that relationship upon the altar as an offering of praise to God?

Your marriage needs to be offered up as a sacrifice every day. So does the way you spend your free time. If you begin to make a list of the things you could offer up in sacrifice, you might never stop writing. You see, the truth is that when your life becomes a temple, a home for Jesus, you begin to see His face in the faces of all those who surround you. You begin to treat them as you would treat Him. You begin to realize that all ground is holy ground because God is there. You begin to see every situation as a potential act of worship, a time to magnify the name of the Lord.

Solitude. Service. Struggles. And ultimately, the one that encapsulates them all: sacrifice. Worship in the midst of these. When that happens, be prepared to throw open the doors of your life. The world is waiting to see the person you will become when you live every moment in the wonder of worship.

LOOK ABOVE FOR HELP

With God nothing will be impossible.

LUKE 1:37

Over and over again in the Old Testament, God is described as the maker of heaven and earth. The Hebrews' worldview was based on the fact that their God was the maker of all things, and as such He had the power and strength to meet all their needs. Therefore it was part of the continual confession, almost as a reminder, that their God (who is also our God) made all things—nothing was too hard for Him.

God created all things, and by Him all things are held together. If God holds the entire universe together, is it not reasonable to assume that He can hold the different aspects of your individual life together as well? He created us for the journey and sustains us through the journey as well.

So when you arrive at a place on your journey and you don't know what to do and you say, "Lord, I need help," remember this: the One to whom you are praying is the One who made heaven and earth. He can help you! The God who created us for life is the One who can help us with life.

David Jeremiah

THERE'S NO SUBSTITUTE FOR GOD'S WORD

We through the patience and comfort of the Scriptures might have hope.

ROMANS 15:4

The Bible is filled with encouraging truths. There's no need to find substitutes from other sources. God's Word is filled with truth, given to us for the sole purpose of encouraging our hearts. In Romans 15, Paul reminds us that one of the purposes of the Old Testament was to provide encouragement for us today: "For whatever things were written before were written for our learning, that we through the patience and comfort [encouragement] of the Scriptures might have hope" (v. 4). Everything from Genesis to Malachi was written for our learning so that we, through the encouragement of the Scriptures, might have hope. If you don't get your encouragement from God's Word, you may find its benefit sadly temporary.

In the New Testament, the theme of encouragement is everywhere, especially in Paul's writings. When Paul wrote to Timothy and Titus, he reminded those young pastors of the critical importance of using God's Word as a tool of encouragement. "Preach the word! Be ready in season and out of season. Convince, rebuke, exhort [encourage], with all longsuffering and teaching" (2 Timothy 4:2).

REDIRECTED FAITH

Not everyone who says to Me, "Lord, Lord," shall enter the kingdom of heaven, but he who does the will of My Father in heaven.

MATTHEW 7:21

Many people believe they will be welcomed into heaven because they've lived a good life, or they come from a religious family, or they've attended church all their lives.

My challenge is to help them see that they are placing faith in themselves—their works, their heritage, their personal standards of ethics and morality, or some other man-made qualification. They haven't understood that, to become a Christian, they must redirect their faith from themselves to Jesus Christ. They must stop trusting in themselves, their parents, their heritage, their morality—and begin trusting in Jesus Christ. They must "bet" their eternal life on Christ alone. They must take Him at His Word that He alone is able to save them.

ANGELS MUST NEVER RECEIVE WORSHIP

Let no one cheat you of your reward, taking delight in false humility and worship of angels, intruding into those things which he has not seen, vainly puffed up by his fleshly mind.

COLOSSIANS 2:18

A desire for angels that is greater than a desire for the Creator will lead to trouble. One reason why angels are invisible to humans may be that, if they were seen, they would be worshiped. Man, who is so prone to idolatry as to worship the works of his own hands, would hardly be able to resist the worship of angels were they before his eyes.

Twice in the book of Revelation, John was confronted by an angel and tried to worship him. Both times the angel told him not to worship the angel but to worship God. Karl Barth once wrote that it is inappropriate for people to talk of angels independent of their experience of God in Christ. While God may send you angels, gratitude must always be directed to God, the God we know in Christ.

It is wrong to "ask your angel" something. We are never told to pray to angels. We pray to God, and He sends the help we need.

WE CAN GO ANYWHERE WITH JESUS

This Book of the Law shall not depart from your mouth, but you shall meditate in it day and night, that you may observe to do according to all that is written in it.

JOSHUA 1:8

Most of us read the Bible casually and carelessly. We read the Word of God, and it has no effect on us. That's why the Word of God has become so insipid in our lives; it has no power over us. The greatest thing we can do in reading God's Word is to understand that the Lord has given the book to us as our marching orders. We are to read it, study it, and then do it. Our prayer before reading the Bible should be, "Lord, show me in Your Word today what You want me to do! Show me the things in my life that are not in conformity with Your will, for I commit myself as I open this book that whatever You say to me here, I'll do it."

With Jesus with us we can go anywhere—into Canaan with its walled cities and giants everywhere, and into the days of the year ahead, where every day poses a mystery and a challenge. We all will face giants in our futures, but know this: if He is with us, we are sufficient to win in the power of our Lord and Savior, Jesus Christ.

David Jeremiah

FROZEN IN SIN

[The wicked man] shall die for lack of instruction, and in the greatness of his folly he shall go astray.

PROVERBS 5:23

The story is told of an eagle perched on a block of ice just above Niagara Falls. The swift current carried the ice and its majestic passenger close to the edge of the great precipice. Other birds warned the eagle of the danger ahead. But their words were unheeded. "I have great and powerful wings," he boasted. "I can fly from my perch at any time."

Suddenly the edge of the falls was only a few feet away. The eagle spread his powerful wings to mount up over his impending doom only to discover that his claws had become frozen to the block of ice.

Scripture warns those who think they are immune to sin to be careful! They are on the verge of falling (1 Corinthians 10:12; 1 Timothy 3:6). "I never thought it would happen to me" are words that have hounded many a person until their dying day (Proverbs 5:11–14). Every Christian needs to know that yielding to temptation can happen—and will, unless the instruction of wisdom is embraced.

Wisdom says, "Hear me clearly: the road to immorality is the road to destruction."

RADER OF THE LOST SOULS

Your ears shall hear a word behind you, saying, "This is the way, walk in it."
ISAIAH 30:21

Evangelist Paul Rader had often spoken to a certain banker in New York concerning his soul, but to no avail. One day God seemed to speak to Rader, urging him to go immediately and once again seek out this individual. Obediently, he caught a train and went to the banker's house. As he approached the house, he saw the banker standing in the doorway. "Oh, Rader," the banker said, "I'm so glad to see you. I wrote a letter begging you to come, but I tore it up."

"That may be so," replied the evangelist, "but your message came by way of heaven." Under deep conviction of sin, the man was impressed by Rader's special effort to reach him with the gospel. Consequently, that very hour he accepted the Lord. In his newfound joy he exclaimed, "Rader, did you ever see the sky so blue or the grass so green?" Suddenly the banker leaned heavily against Rader, then with a gasp fell into his arms—dead! He had been saved on the very brink of eternity. What if Paul Rader had delayed to come, taking the promptings of the Lord with less urgency? Let us always be keenly sensitive to the Lord's leadings.

THE SPIRIT'S INSTRUCTION

Now we have received, not the spirit of the world, but the Spirit who is from God, that we might know the things that have been freely given to us by God.

1 CORINTHIANS 2:12

Years ago, I remember hearing Campus Crusade founder Bill Bright teaching on the Holy Spirit. In his message, he told about a man to whom he'd been witnessing. One of this man's problems with the Christian faith was that he'd tried again and again to read the Bible but couldn't make any sense of it.

Then the man received Jesus Christ and came back to visit Dr. Bright a week later. He had an amazing story to tell. During that week's time, he said, it was as though somebody had rewritten his Bible. Suddenly the Scripture came alive to him. Understanding broke into his thoughts like quick lightning strikes.

How had it happened? The Teacher had taken up residence within him. What had once been obscure and confusing now pulsated with meaning, encouragement, and hope.

Paul wrote, "Now we have received, not the spirit of the world, but the Spirit who is from God, that we might know the things that have been freely given to us by God." That means that Christians, who have the Spirit of God living within them, have an inward interpreter who helps them to understand what the Bible means.

WAITING OUT OF CONTROL

Abram fell on his face, and God talked with him, saying, "As for Me, behold, My covenant is with you, and you shall be a father of many nations."

GENESIS 17:3–4

We learn from reading about Abraham that hope is necessary because often waiting is uncontrollable. Did you know God didn't tell him how long he would have to wait? He just said, "Here's the hope. You just wait."

God's promise to Abraham was not to be fulfilled for many years. And in some respects that promise was not totally fulfilled even in his lifetime. You and I are the fulfillment of that promise. According to Galatians, we are the children of Abraham. We are the result of God having blessed Abraham, Isaac, and Jacob; having blessed the nation of Israel; and then, through Israel, having blessed all of us. We are blessed because of Abraham. But Abraham never saw all of that. He saw enough, but he had to wait.

Hope is the ingredient that keeps us going between the promise and the fulfillment. Hope is the thing that gets us up in the morning when we know that God cares but we haven't seen any evidence of it in the last few days. Hope drives us onward when we want to stop and quit. Hope keeps our dreams alive while we are waiting. And we need hope because we can't always control the timetable.

David Jeremiah

AWESTRUCK

Who shall not fear You, O Lord, and glorify Your name? For you alone are holy.
REVELATION 15:4

The primary meaning of the word *holy* is "separate." It means "to cut." A holy person is cut apart from the rest. God is holy in that He is totally, in His person, separate from all of us. So much so that it is almost a foreign subject to talk of Him. He is so awesome and so overwhelming in His person that there is nothing in human language or in human experience to which we may compare Him.

Some years ago, a German scholar named Rudolf Otto tried to determine in a scientific way what happened to people when they came in contact with that which they believed to be holy. He observed that there is something extra in the experience of the Holy, something you can't describe in human terms. The clearest sensation a human being has when he experiences the Holy is an overwhelming sense of creatureliness. When we meet the Absolute, we know immediately that we are not absolute. When we meet the Infinite, we come in contact immediately with our own finiteness. When we meet the Absolute Holy, we become aware that we are not like that.

JULY

*Therefore, having been justified by faith, we have peace
with God through our Lord Jesus Christ.*

—ROMANS 5:1

OFFERING OF PEACE

Peace I leave with you, My peace I give to you.

JOHN 14:27

Christ offered His peace to the disciples during an unbelievably difficult period in His own life. He was enjoying the peace of God, but He knew the disciples were about to be sorely tested and would need God's peace as well. Anyone can have peace when things are going well at home, with finances, and with regard to health. Even the world can manifest a semblance of peace when everything is going smoothly.

It is in the context of difficulties that God wants us to experience His peace and manifest it to the world. Jesus offered His peace to the disciples at exactly the time it would be needed most: a time when their own sense of peace and calm would likely disappear. He wanted His disciples—and He wants us—to be at peace during the most difficult hours of our lives.

Believers in Christ can live in a world where seemingly irrational and indiscriminate things happen without warning but not be undone by worry and fear. We can have peace knowing that God is in control of our lives. While it may appear that things are out of control in the world, we can know that we are eternally protected and watched over by God's sovereign and loving care.

David Jeremiah

WORSHIP COURAGEOUSLY

I will praise You with my whole heart; before the gods I will sing praises to You.
PSALM 138:1

David was not ashamed of his God. He would boldly praise the God of Israel in the presence of false gods without worrying what anyone said or thought of him. Are you willing to do that today?

I can remember when it was very common to see families and others in restaurants bowing their heads and joining hands to worship and thank God before their meal. Our family does that, but I don't see as many today as I used to. It is a wonderful way to encourage other families. People who are not ashamed to pray publicly to their God stand out in an age when it is common to be ridiculed for your faith.

I see some people who sort of bow their head, or look like they're looking for their napkin, or scratch their forehead—trying to pray before their meal without looking like they're praying. Who are they fooling? David said, "I will praise my God before all the pagan gods." He praised God courageously.

CARING FOR SINGLE SAINTS

Now all who believed were together, and had all things in common, and sold their possessions and goods, and divided them among all, as anyone had need.

ACTS 2:44–45

I want to address a word to single parents—and to those in the churches they attend. I know of no greater need for a ministry of support and encouragement than to those who are handling the pressures and responsibilities of vocation and childrearing alone. Single parents are fighting battles that no one else in the church is facing.

God can use our resources to help meet the needs of the single parents in our churches. He wants to use people to meet the needs of people in our churches today—especially the needs of all our single saints.

Are you a single Christian? Then do what you can to express a desire for ministry and a desire to be ministered to. If you are a leader in your church, do what you can to raise the priority and resources given to ministry to singles. This growing segment of the church must no longer feel as though they are outsiders. They must be as welcome as the most famous single person of all time—Jesus Himself.

David Jeremiah

SPIRITUAL LIBERTY

*God has not given us a spirit of fear, but of power and of love
and of a sound mind.*

2 TIMOTHY 1:7

We have been released from the spirit of fear by
the Holy Spirit, who has placed us in the body of
Christ. We have received the Spirit of adoption. This adoption provides for every believer release from the bondage
that he once knew. The picture that Paul uses is the contrast
between slavery and sonship. Slavery, with its fear and isola-
tion, stands for our old lives before knowing Christ. We are
told by the writer of Hebrews that Christ died that He might
destroy the one who had the power of death and release those
who were subject to a fear of death (Hebrews 2:14–15). The
perfect love of God has cast out the fear to which we were
once enslaved (2 Timothy 1:7; 1 John 4:18).

Anything that involves a believer in fear of bondage cannot possibly be the work of the Holy Spirit of God. It must
come either from his own heart of unbelief or as a temptation of the evil one. Our sonship implies perfect spiritual
liberty and the absence of all legal features that would bring
us once more under the law.

BOAST ABOUT GOD

My soul shall make its boast in the Lord.

PSALM 34:2

When I feel afraid, I'm prone to pull the blanket over my head and hope it goes away. Or I nurse my fears. The adversary of our souls loves to get our attention focused on ourselves and not on the resources of our God.

What will happen when you praise and worship God? Your praise makes God big in your heart and mind. Soon, your problem falls into perspective. When I worship God, sometimes even with the tears coming down my face, my spirit is renewed as I praise God. My problem doesn't go away, but all of a sudden I see it in relation to the One who is in charge of everything.

It's interesting what we boast about, isn't it? At the last party you went to, what did you boast about? Put the spotlight on the Lord, and focus on Him. When we get together with friends, let's just brag on Jesus. So many good things are happening in our lives as individuals, in our families, and in our churches that we ought to boast on the Lord all the time.

David Jeremiah

KEEP THE FAITH

It is required in stewards that one be found faithful.

I CORINTHIANS 4:2

God places a high premium on the quality of faithfulness. He says to us by way of Paul in I Corinthians 4:2, "It is required in stewards that one be found faithful." We are all stewards of the grace of God. God has given Christians an opportunity to administer part of His kingdom on this earth on His behalf.

If there is anything at all we need in our churches, it is this quality of faithfulness. Sometimes described as fidelity, sometimes defined as steadfastness, it always means the determination to stay by your word and complete your commitment.

How we need the quality of faithfulness in our world today. Contracts mean nothing. Commitments mean nothing. We don't mean what we say. Sooner or later, like everything else, that kind of thing begins to creep into the body of Christ. We have lost the characteristic of faithfulness.

God is teaching us that we are to be faithful no matter what. What a freeing thing that is! God has given all of us something to do, and He says to us, "Here's what I want from you in this assignment. Be faithful."

JESUS' FINAL WARNING

Take heed to yourselves and to all the flock, among which the Holy Spirit has made you overseers, to shepherd the church of God which He purchased with His own blood.

ACTS 20:28

If AT&T could establish a direct phone link between earth and heaven on a given Sunday morning and Jesus spoke simultaneously via satellite to congregations all over the world, what do you think He would say? You're sitting there in your pew, your heart beating fast. What will His instructions be? "You shall be witnesses to Me . . . to the end of the earth." And after He said that, I think He would certainly repeat the words He spoke to Peter: "Feed my sheep."

In other words, "Brothers and sisters in the church, you live in a time of terrible demolition. My eyes miss nothing. I have seen it all. But even while precious things all around you are being torn down and dismantled, you can be in the process of building. Build up My church! Take care of My sheep. Feed them. Tend them. Love them . . . as I have loved you."

We don't need a direct phone line, do we? We don't need a satellite connection to heaven. He has given us His inerrant Word, which is a light to our feet and a lamp to our path. He has given us His Holy Spirit to dwell within us, illuminating the pages of Scripture, reminding us of everything Jesus taught.

David Jeremiah

THE SPIRIT OF ENCOURAGEMENT

The Helper, the Holy Spirit, whom the Father will send in My name,
He will teach you all things, and bring to your remembrance all the
things that I said to you.

JOHN 14:26

The Holy Spirit's other name is Comforter. That is my favorite name for the Holy Spirit. The word *comforter* is a Greek word, *paraclete*, and it is the same word that is translated "encourager."

The Holy Spirit is my Encourager. He comes and puts His arm around me when I am discouraged, and He encourages me.

Yes, there are times when this pastor loses his perspective a little and becomes discouraged. I may have actually slipped into depression once or twice (not recently, thank the Lord). It's the same with anyone in leadership; sometimes you feel as though there is hardly anywhere to run. You just have to get alone with your Bible, get down on your knees in prayer . . . and then the Spirit of God comes to bring encouragement to your heart. I've had that experience time and again. It is almost (almost!) worth experiencing the dark and heavy times because the encouragement of God's Spirit is so sweet. I praise God that the Holy Spirit is my Comforter and Encourager and Helper.

TRIALS IN THE BELIEVER'S LIFE

Deliver me in Your righteousness, and cause me to escape; incline
Your ear to me and save me.

PSALM 71:2

When in the hospital during my bout with cancer, I awakened in a morphine-induced grogginess with the thought to read Psalm 71. I recall noting the hour—3:00 a.m.—but could not remember who, prior to coming to the hospital, had encouraged me to meditate on that particular psalm. I reached for my Bible and began to read the words of the psalmist, who wrote concerning a dark night he had been through. The words of that psalm were a bright light in a dark night in my life—and can be for you as well.

Regardless of the name of the author of this psalm, we do know this about him: he was thoroughly familiar with the ways and words of God. It is a compilation of truths about God's deliverance of His saints during times of trouble.

It is not the absence of suffering but the response to suffering that makes Christians unique. Believers are not exempt from trials in life, but we can be exempt from failure in those trials.

David Jeremiah

Doing the Right Thing

Wisdom is the principal thing; therefore get wisdom: and in all your getting, get understanding.

Proverbs 4:7

My favorite secular definition of *wisdom* is, "Doing the right thing without precedent." That means you know what to do in a situation even though you've never experienced it before.

In his book *Knowing God*, J. I. Packer offers a helpful illustration for understanding wisdom using the metaphor of a railroad or subway system. He said some people think of wisdom as if they're sitting in the control room looking at a giant board on which the movement of all the trains is tracked. You can see everything that's going on in the city's rail system at one time; you have a total picture of everything. Some people think the wiser they become the greater grasp they will have of the mysteries of God—how everything in the universe works and how all the pieces fit together. But that is not what biblical wisdom is all about.

I have found the opposite to be true. The more knowledge of God I get (that is, the wiser I become), the more I realize how much I don't know, and will never know, about God and His ways.

No Ministry Apart from Service

As each one has received a gift, minister it to one another, as good stewards of the manifold grace of God.

1 Peter 4:10

Ministry and *service* are from the same Greek word and mean essentially the same thing. There is no ministry apart from service. No one can have an impact in ministry who is not also willing to serve or to be a servant.

There is always a price tag attached to service. It might be health; it might be convenience; it might be aggravation; it might be humility. Whatever the cost, it is what adorns the neck of those who minister.

Ministry in the church is like being a parent. The most successful parents are those who learn to sacrifice for their children. And while we parents think our children are never going to realize what we have sacrificed in service to them, they eventually do. And what we have sacrificed for them comes back to us as the fruit of a close and intimate relationship with them. And it's the same way in ministry in the church. The more we give of ourselves in ministry to others, the more we will get back in return. I heard the speaker John Maxwell say once, "If you are going to go up, you have to give up." There is no way to advance in ministry without giving of ourselves.

David Jeremiah

ARE YOU GOOD?

Why do you call Me good? No one is good but One, that is, God.
MATTHEW 19:17

A person who is a good person is an individual of lofty ideals, noble purposes, strong character, reliable conduct and trustworthy integrity. The only one who truly embodies all of those characteristics is Jesus Christ.

We come to understand the word *goodness* as we see it alongside the word *righteousness*. Someone has said that justice is what God gives to us that we deserve. Goodness goes beyond that and is that which God gives us beyond what we deserve.

The great characteristic of goodness as it is found in relationship with righteousness is generosity. It is what a person gets that isn't deserved. It is what God gives to a person that could never be earned. Goodness in its relationship to righteousness teaches us about generosity.

You don't have to be rich to be generous. But what do you do with what you have? We need to take a good, long look at our lives and ask God how our attitudes have been to the needs around us. If we've been protective and closefisted, we need to say, "God, by the grace You will give me, I will change." Begin to bear fruit in your life, the fruit of a generous spirit.

PRAYER CIRCLES

Be anxious for nothing, but in everything by prayer and supplication, with thanksgiving, let your requests be made known to God.

PHILIPPIANS 4:6

One of the best ways I know to remember how to commit things to God in prayer is by remembering three circles. One is the worry circle, in which I keep *nothing*. Second is the prayer circle, in which I keep *everything*. Third is the gratitude circle, in which I keep *anything*. So when I pray, I am anxious for *nothing*, prayerful for *everything*, and thankful for *anything* (Philippians 4:6).

We feel foolish asking God to help us with some of the things in our lives. But remember: "In *everything* by prayer and supplication, with thanksgiving, let your requests be made known to God." You just need to write out every one of your concerns before they turn into worries and commit them to God. He does care about each of them. If you take them back, just give them back to Him in prayer again. Day by day, as you get more and more practiced at committing the affairs of your life to Him, you will begin to leave them with Him. Your trust in Him will grow, and you will stop grabbing back what you have given Him.

David Jeremiah

FOOTPRINTS

Fear not, for I am with you.

ISAIAH 43:5

While stranded on a deserted island, Daniel Defoe's character, Robinson Crusoe, salvaged a Bible from the shipwreck, read it, and was converted. He grew into a devout Christian. His life, though missing human companionship, was peaceful and prayerful.

But one day he found a footprint in the sand and realized he wasn't alone. Knowing the cannibalism of the local tribes, he grew into a fearful man, looking over his shoulder with every step. He no longer slept peacefully. He altered his habits. He visualized himself being captured and devoured. "That former confidence in God . . . now vanished, as if He that had fed me by miracle hitherto could not preserve, by His power, the provision which He had made for me by His goodness."

Crusoe had to go back to his Bible, repent of anxiety, and be strengthened again in his faith. He eventually learned the great lesson of faltering Christians: the things we most fear are likely, in the providence of God, to be most used for our good. In the end, those footprints led to his deliverance.

God has planned out our future from eternity past and guaranteed it with His promises. We can trust Him.

A SURE HOPE

Christ in you, the hope of glory.

COLOSSIANS 1:27

Though World War II did not officially end until 1945, it can be safely said that it was over on June 6, 1944. That was D-day, when 176,000 Allied troops stormed the beaches of Normandy in France. Eventually, three-quarters of a million troops assembled in France to liberate Europe from the Axis powers led by Adolf Hitler. Many fierce battles followed D-day before the Axis armies were defeated. But the die was cast on D-day when hope came once again to the free world.

The same may be said of our Christian experience. Though the day is yet in the future when evil will be eradicated from earth completely, we know it will happen because of the death and resurrection of Jesus Christ. By His death, Christ freed believers from the debt of sin. And by His resurrection, death, the last great enemy, was conquered so we might live again and forever. Are you in a battle or skirmish today with the world, the flesh, or the devil? Don't wish things were different. Instead, put your hope in the fact that with the invasion of Christ into this world, victory was won. True hope is available to all allies of the conquering Christ. True hope is not wishful thinking; it is faith in fact.

GOD'S HAT TRICK

A man's heart plans his way, but the LORD directs his steps.

PROVERBS 16:9

Richard Storrs and Gordon Hall were students at the same theological seminary. One Saturday near the end of the semester, Hall was preparing to go to Braintree, Massachusetts, to preach, hoping that he might receive an invitation to become their pastor. That afternoon as he was splitting some wood, his hat fell beneath the axe and was destroyed. He didn't have the money to replace it and the weather was bitter cold, so he asked his friend to take the assignment. Storrs preached and was offered the job. He accepted it, and he remained the minister of that parish until his dying day—a period of more than half a century!

Hall, although disappointed, sought other outlets for his talents. He went to India and became the first American missionary to Bombay. He was quite influential in the Indian missions movement. No one who believes in divine providence will for a moment doubt that God stationed Storrs at Braintree and Hall in India. By means of that ruined hat, the courses of two lives were changed. Nevertheless, in God's divine will, the good news was proclaimed.

SET FREE

He made Him who knew no sin to be sin for us, that we might become the righteousness of God in Him.

2 CORINTHIANS 5:21

I once heard someone say that of all men who ever lived, Barabbas should have the best understanding of vicarious substitution. Somebody died in his place. This murderer and thief walked out a free man, the crowds cheering his release. At the same time, an innocent Jesus was sentenced to die.

But Barabbas isn't the only one who can say that Jesus died in his place. We can all say that Jesus Christ died on that cross for us, just as He did for Barabbas. In the words of 2 Corinthians 5:21, "For He made Him who knew no sin to be sin for us, that we might become the righteousness of God in Him." Jesus died that we might live. He was bound that we who are in bondage to sin might be set free.

When word of his freedom came, he had to walk out of that cell to be truly free. Through Christ, the cell door has sprung open. All we have to do is say, "I accept what Christ did for me, and I will now live in the light of that truth."

David Jeremiah

WORSHIP INTELLIGENTLY

I will . . . praise Your name for Your loving kindness and Your truth; for You have magnified Your word above all Your name. In the day when I cried out, You answered me.

PSALM 138:2–3

D avid notes three things for which we are to praise God when we are in trouble. These make a great outline for praying in times of trouble.

1. *Praise Him for His mercy and truth.* God is perfectly balanced in mercy and in truth. When you come to Him, His truth is tempered by mercy and His mercy is illumined by truth.

2. *Praise Him for His magnified Word.* When you read God's Word and read of His loving-kindness and truth, you can know that the integrity of God and His name are behind those words.

3. *Praise Him for His mighty provision.* Whatever His answer, it gives us strength that makes us bold. And boldness allows us to face troubles without fear. We face trouble with confidence and strength, knowing that God is with us and will see us through. That kind of perspective keeps us from cowering in the corners of life and gives us the confidence to face each day unafraid of what it might bring.

THE STRONG TOWER

The name of the LORD is a strong tower; the righteous run to it and are safe.

PROVERBS 18:10

On January 25, 1934, German clergyman Martin Neimoller confronted Adolph Hitler face-to-face in the name of Christ. As a result, Neimoller was later seized by the Gestapo and held in solitary confinement.

On the morning of his trial, he was led from his cell by a green-uniformed official. As the two men walked through eerie underground passageways, Neimoller felt overwhelming fear.

Suddenly he heard a whispered voice: "The name of the Lord is a strong tower. The righteous run to it and are safe." It was the guard, speaking under his breath.

With those words, Neimoller's fear vanished. It was replaced by an indescribable peace that didn't leave him, even during the dark days to come.

The Bible warns that prior to Christ's return the days will be perilous (2 Timothy 3:1). But even when things seem to be in chaos around us, the name of our Lord is a strong tower. The righteous run to it and are safe. God's purpose will guide us, His promises will sustain us, and His providence will keep us.

David Jeremiah

FORGIVENESS IN MARRIAGE

If you have anything against anyone, forgive him.
MARK 11:25

It's impossible to have a good marriage without learning how to forgive because it's impossible to have a marriage without hurting one another. Why? Because both partners are flawed human beings. Someone has said that the six most important words in a marriage are, "I admit I made a mistake." Do you know how hard it is to say those words?

Forgiveness is at the very core of relationships within the home and within the church. Whether someone has something against us or we have something against another, we are to be the proactive ones and forgive, restoring the relationship. In an ideal world, when there had been some discord or hurt in a marriage, a husband and wife ought to run into each other as they are both going to seek the forgiveness of the other, restoring harmony in the relationship.

Can you imagine a marriage that would not prosper if it were built on communication and conversation that is trustworthy, gentle, open, kind, and forgiving? While staying married is a worthy goal, a better goal is to be married—and happily so!

ABSOLUTE LOVE

Rejoice with the wife of your youth.

PROVERBS 5:18

How do you recover a lost love? Go back to the beginning of the relationship, and ask yourself, "What was I doing then that I'm not doing now?" and do it. Take her some flowers. I guarantee she will like it. She'll feel better because you did it, and you'll feel better too.

If you aren't all the way gone, if it's not too late for you, if there's any hope at all, you'll discover all kinds of things that you feel better for doing. The love that should be in your heart toward the woman who is your wife will begin to develop according to your loving activities. We husbands are responsible to be the leaders in love in our families. That's what it means to be the head. We are to be like Christ.

When we try to love our marriage partners realistically, sacrificially, purposefully, willingly, and absolutely, we begin to come into God's plan. And without thinking of it or planning for it, we find our own needs being met too. Our realistic, sacrificial, purposeful, willing, absolute love comes back to us from our partners, and that is the payoff. Even though Christ has not promised us lives of ease without struggle or pain, He has promised us joy.

David Jeremiah

THE POWER OF A MOTHER

His mother kept all these things in her heart.

LUKE 2:51

The person who most influenced John Wesley, the founder of Methodism, was likely his mother, Susanna. She was fiercely devoted to the ten of her eighteen children who survived infancy, spending time with a different child each night of the week to school him or her in matters of the faith. In a letter to his mother as an adult, Wesley said, "Oh, Mother, what I'd give for a Thursday evening!" When John and Charles Wesley consulted their mother before going to America as missionaries in 1735, she said, "If I had twenty sons, I should rejoice if they were all so employed, though I should never see them more."

It has been suggested that the discipline and love of Susanna Wesley's household was formative in shaping the structure of early Methodism through her influence on John and Charles. How powerful is the influence of a mother! The bond between mother and child seems to be God-designed, the perfect union of potential and the power to make it spring forth. The simple, daily influences of prayer, persuasion, and promoting of godly values are the most powerful tools a mother can use to unleash the potential of her children.

PATIENCE, ANYONE?

For this reason I obtained mercy, that in me first Jesus Christ might show all longsuffering, as a pattern to those who are going to believe on Him for everlasting life.

1 TIMOTHY 1:16

You've probably heard the great American prayer: "God give me patience, and I want it *now*!" We are constantly being reminded that everything can be done in a hurry, yet God says He wants to teach us to wait.

God wants to develop within us a quality of being patient and long-suffering. Someone has defined long-suffering as a long holding out of the mind before it gives way to action or passion. It is the power to see things through.

If there is any quality we need in our lives today, it is patience. It is the hardest of all the qualities for us to learn today because we think everything has to be done quickly. But it is the virtue I believe is closest to the heart of God. God is a God of long-suffering, patience, and forbearance.

A person who has the fruit of long-suffering is patient with people who nag. He or she does not criticize and irritate when criticized and irritated. This person does not disappear when frustrated or angered. Long-suffering knows how to sit still and wait its turn. It is slow to retaliate and does not seek to get even. It waits patiently with joy.

David Jeremiah

A PAID FRIEND

*You also may have fellowship with us; and truly our fellowship is with the
Father and with His Son Jesus Christ.*

1 JOHN 1:3

A famous British playwright was leaving Liverpool by
ship. He noticed that the other passengers were waving to friends on the dock. Just before the ship was to leave,
he rushed down to the dock and stopped a little boy. "Would
you wave to me if I pay you?" he asked the boy. "Of course,"
he agreed. The writer gave him a few shillings, then ran back
aboard and leaned over the rail. Sure enough, the boy was
waving to him. The playwright disliked solitude and loneliness so much that he had gone so far as to create an artificial
friend. To him, even the semblance of friendship was better
than the crushing loneliness he felt.

The key to assurance in life is fellowship. Fellowship
with people locks out the grim feelings of loneliness. And
fellowship with God keeps away the threat of eternal solitude.

In this epistle, John wanted to make it clear to his
readers that they could fellowship with God through Jesus
Christ. He stressed the importance of love: since Christians
have experienced the love of God in their lives, they have no
need to fear either in this life or in the life to come.

SUFFERING TO BLESS OTHERS

Do not lose heart at my tribulations for you, which is your glory.

EPHESIANS 3:13

Sometimes we discover that a major reason for our suffering has been what God intended to do in someone else's life. That may not be obvious to us. But Paul says that his sufferings were for the glory (or means of blessing) of others (Ephesians 3:13).

"But I want you to know, brethren, that the things which happened to me have actually turned out for the furtherance of the gospel, so that it has become evident to the whole palace guard, and to all the rest, that my chains are in Christ; and most of the brethren in the Lord, having become confident by my chains, are much more bold to speak the word without fear" (Philippians 1:12–14).

We do not always see the realization of God's purposes. None of us has the ability to interpret God's perfectly wise purpose in the sufferings of our fellow believers (or of ourselves for that matter). But in order to encourage them, we need to have some awareness of what God may be doing. By sharing the biblical teaching on what God does in our lives through suffering, we may encourage others to serve God in it.

David Jeremiah

FATHER–SON TALKS

The fear of the LORD is the beginning of knowledge, but fools despise wisdom and instruction.

PROVERBS 1:7

Mark Twain is given credit for the following remark: "When I was a boy of fourteen, my father was so ignorant I could hardly stand to have the old man around. But when I got to be twenty-one, I was astonished at how much the old man had learned in seven years." If that were a true record of a young man's awakening to wisdom, Mark Twain would not be the first to whom it happened. Many a young man has listened to advice from his father and discounted it—until the day he needed it. Then it turned out to be more wisdom than advice.

One of the oldest father–son talks in history is recorded in the book of Proverbs. Solomon, the world's wisest man in his day (and likely in ours), used his throne as king of Israel to dispense his wise sayings to his subjects and to those who came from afar to sit at his feet and learn. Solomon was known throughout the surrounding nations for possessing uncanny wisdom, discernment, and insight.

The principles of wisdom will work for anyone who puts them to use. But it is only those who fear the Lord who will want to practice them over a lifetime.

GOD'S PLAN FOR THE HOME

There is neither Jew nor Greek, there is neither slave nor free, there is neither male nor female; for you are all one in Christ Jesus.

GALATIANS 3:28

Galatians 3:28 makes it absolutely clear that men and women stand equal in privilege and position before God. In God's sight, there is no male and female; there are only those created in His image who are redeemed and placed into the body of Christ. In the church of Jesus Christ, we all submit to one another—bond or free, Jew or Gentile, male or female. That is the clear intention of God, for there is one Lord over all in the church to whom we submit.

But when it comes to the functioning and the operation of the Christian home, God has given guidelines so that the home will work according to order and according to His plan. He has said, "I'm going to give you the joy of personal relationships within the context of a loving environment called the home," which He established in the garden of Eden. And He said, "Here's how I want this to work. I want the husband to be the lover and the learner and the leader, and I want the wife to be supportive and submissive in that relationship. When you do that, there will be blessing, joy, and honor, and it will be an exciting experience."

David Jeremiah

STRENGTH!

I pray that out of his glorious riches he may strengthen you with power through his Spirit in your inner being.

EPHESIANS 3:16 NIV

From one end of the Bible to the other, we read of God's strengthening His people. When the Israelites passed through the Red Sea, they praised the Lord, saying: "The LORD is my strength and my song" (Exodus 15:2 NIV).

Deuteronomy 33:25 says: "As your days, so shall your strength be." Nehemiah 8:10 says, "Do not sorrow for the joy of the LORD is your strength." Psalm 27:1 declares, "The Lord is my light and my salvation. Whom shall I fear? The Lord is the strength of my life; of whom shall I be afraid? Psalm 46:1 avows, "God is our refuge and strength, a very present help in trouble."

Isaiah said, "Trust in the Lord forever, for in YAH, the Lord, is everlasting strength" (26:4). Isaiah 40:31 promises that "those who wait on the Lord shall renew their strength; they shall mount up with wings like eagles, they shall run and not be weary, they shall walk and not faint."

The apostle Paul told us to "be strong in the Lord and in the power of His might" (Ephesians 6:10). "I can do all things through Christ who strengthens me," he said in Philippians 4:13.

Throughout the Bible we find a simple formula: when the Word goes in, praise goes up, and faith goes out, God goes forth to strengthen His people.

THERE IS ONLY ONE BUILDER

Unless the LORD builds the house, they labor in vain who build it.

PSALM 127:1

If you are going to be successful in building a family, you have to place God at the head of your home. The psalmist says in Psalm 127:1, "Unless the LORD builds the house, they labor in vain who build it." This is the most important truth in building a home. It's saying if God doesn't build it, it isn't going to work. There is only one builder in the home, and that builder is God. God, who had the idea of the home, is the One who wants to be at the head of the home. Until God is at the center of your home, all your attempts at making family life what you want will be attempts in frustration. Unless you let Him build the home, you're going to do it in vain.

We communicate our values where they really are. The best thing we could do before we install God at the head of the home is to install Him at the head of our life. Then we can ask Him to live that out little by little in our families.

David Jeremiah

PEACE, PLEASE

Therefore, having been justified by faith, we have peace with God through our Lord Jesus Christ.

ROMANS 5:1

True peace gives not only a calm exterior, but a very quiet inside as well. Peace seems to be an elusive quality that everyone chases after and few people find. Romans 5:1 says, "Therefore, having been justified by faith, we have peace with God." What does that mean? Is God my enemy? Have I been at war with God? God is holy and humans are sinful. They are on different sides. As creatures apart from God, we are at enmity with God.

But the Bible says God provided Jesus Christ that we might have peace with God. I see that picture so beautifully illustrated by the cross itself. Pointing up to heaven, it pictures that Jesus Christ, the God-man, reached up and took the hand of the Father. Pointing down toward earth, it pictures that Jesus Christ, the Son of man, reached down and took hold of fallen human beings. With one hand in the hand of God and the other hand in the hand of man, the only unique personality who was God and man brought the two together and made peace between God and man. He is our peace. He is the Prince of Peace because He is the One who solved the enmity between us and God. Accept Him and you have peace with God.

GAINING PERSPECTIVE

Faith comes by hearing, and hearing by the word of God.

ROMANS 10:17

It's impossible to have faith unless the mind embraces that information that comprises the gospel message. There are specific facts that must be embraced. Faith is not just a warm feeling that comes over you on a bright, sunny day. How would anyone in Seattle or Alaska ever get saved? No, faith is more than a warm feeling. It is the appropriation of certain facts about a man named Jesus.

Gaining perception means you have perceived something. And that "something" is the facts of the gospel message—objective, quantifiable, expressible information. The Bible speaks about false gospels, which means someone has the facts wrong, purposefully or accidentally. So the truth is what has to be perceived and received as "step one" in gaining faith. And that truth comes by hearing the Word of God.

David Jeremiah

AUGUST

*These things I have spoken to you, that My joy may
remain in you, and that your joy may be full.*

—JOHN 15:11

GOD DESERVES ATTENTION

I will meditate on Your precepts, and contemplate Your ways.

PSALM 119:15

Most of us don't spend a lot of time thinking about God. We go to church on Sunday and we sing the songs and we talk the way Christians talk, but we don't give God the attention He deserves. We don't give Him the concentrated attention of someone who is trying to get to know and get close to another person. But a relationship with God is similar to a relationship with a person. If we want to have a meaningful relationship, we must spend time getting to know that person. We must spend time talking with and listening to that person. We can't be close to someone if we don't know who they really are.

God tells us in the Bible who He is. Not only that, but He tells us how much He wants us to know Him.

The more you know God, the more you will love Him. And the more you know and love Him, the more you can celebrate Him in the way He deserves.

David Jeremiah

HE STRETCHES OUT HIS HAND

*Though I walk in the midst of trouble, You will revive me; You will stretch out
Your hand against the wrath of my enemies, and Your right hand will save me.*

PSALM 138:7

David spent most of his life in trouble. Before he is king he is running from Saul; as king he is warring with his neighbors. And toward the end of his reign, his house rises up in rebellion against him. David walked most of his life in the midst of trouble. Yet David said in Psalm 23, "Yea, though I walk through the valley of the shadow of death, I will fear no evil; for You are with me; Your rod and Your staff, they comfort me" (v. 4). David was confident of God's protection, just as David's sheep had been "confident" of David's protection when he was their shepherd in the Judean hills.

Does that mean we will never be injured? Apparently not, for David says God will "revive" him when needed. But it does mean that God will proactively stretch out His hand in our behalf. He will protect us.

PRAYER IS HARD WORK

Epaphras, who is one of you, a bondservant of Christ, greets you, always laboring fervently for you in prayers, that you may stand perfect and complete in all the will of God.

COLOSSIANS 4:12

Fiercely is the right English word to convey Paul's meaning here. He says Epaphras labors fervently in prayer, and the word *laboring* is sometimes translated as "wrestling." The image is that of Greek athletes who competed fiercely to win a perishable crown of an olive leaf garland. And in our modern day, how many athletes devote years of their lives to preparing for the Olympic games? The sacrifices they endure and the prices they pay are almost inconceivable to the non–Olympically inclined among us. They train and compete fiercely, pushing themselves beyond the limits of endurance.

One of the greatest revelations I've had in recent years is that prayer is hard work. Prayer requires labor, striving, continuance, endurance, wrestling, and faithfulness. I've heard people say, "I would pray more, but it's so hard." At least they understood the nature of prayer. It is indeed hard work. Sometimes it helps to begin our prayers by confessing we don't feel like praying—and ask God to help us with our preference to be doing something else. Be honest with God and ask Him to give you a willingness to do the work of prayer.

David Jeremiah

NEED A FRIEND?

A friend loves at all times, and a brother is born for adversity.

PROVERBS 17:17

I believe God intends relationships and friendships to be the context in which He does some of His most important work in our lives. Life is difficult from any perspective, and everyone needs friends to help them through the difficult times. Those who have close friends know they couldn't live without them. Friends love you enough to confront you when you are wrong and to stand by you through thick and thin. These are friends who act toward you like a marriage partner is supposed to—for better or for worse. If you have a friend like that, you are rich. If you have more than one, you are wealthy beyond measure. In today's world, many people do not take time to cultivate committed friendships, and they are the poorer for it. But the need for committed friends doesn't mean we should rush out and try to accumulate them on a wholesale basis. Many things in life are not left to our choosing, but friendships are. The choice of friends is more than a right, however—it is a responsibility.

RIGHTEOUSNESS IS A FREE GIFT

For Christ is the end of the law for righteousness to everyone who believes.

ROMANS 10:4

C hrist did in His perfect flesh what the flesh of mortal man could never do—keep the law of God. There is nothing wrong with the law; it is just and holy and good (Romans 7:12).

The problem is sinful human flesh. We have no ability to keep God's holy Law. And if one is going to establish his own righteousness, it means keeping 100 percent of God's requirements according to the law. To break the law in one point is to break it all (James 2:10). Therefore Christ came into the world to do what we could not do—satisfy the requirements of the law in order to win righteousness for those who would receive it as a free gift instead of trying to earn it themselves.

Christ is the end of righteousness for all who believe. Are you one who has believed? If so, let your life become an "I love You" to God, thanking Him for what Christ has done for you.

David Jeremiah

ARE YOU A JOYLESS CHRISTIAN?

The kingdom of God is . . . righteousness and peace and joy in the Holy Spirit.
ROMANS 14:17

I f you're a Christian and you don't have joy, here are some very basic things you need to understand about what it means to have the joy of the Lord in your life. Receiving Christ, submitting to the Spirit, reading the Bible, and praying don't sound very original. But there isn't anything more original than the Word of God. That's the bedrock simplicity of what it means to have joy in Christ. Here is why: if joy is in Christ, then everything that has to do with joy has to be centered on Christ.

As the Holy Spirit indwells and controls us, and as we read the Bible, we will come to prayer time and into fellowship with Jesus. As we spend time with Him, we come to love, adore, and praise Him, and Jesus becomes literally the focus of our lives. That is how we have joy in God.

Christian joy isn't always laughing and having a good, hilarious time. Christian joy is the deep, settled peace that comes to live within your heart when you know that the really important things are all right. Life can be taken from us, but we are going to live somewhere for eternity. You can have joy in your heart when you know everything is all right with you forever.

ETERNAL PROTECTION

Having now been justified by His blood, we shall be saved from wrath through Him.

ROMANS 5:9

The story is told of a man who had been condemned by a Spanish court to be shot. Because he was an American citizen and of English birth, the consuls of the United States and England decided to intervene. They declared that the Spanish authorities had no power to put him to death. Their protest went unheeded, and the Spaniards proceeded to prepare the firing squad.

At the time the execution was scheduled to take place, the consuls boldly approached the accused man, already tied and blindfolded, and wrapped him up in their flags—the Stars and Stripes and the Union Jack. Then they shouted, "Fire a shot if you dare! If you do so, you will bring the powers of our two great empires upon you." There stood the prisoner, unharmed. One bullet could have ended his life, but protected by those flags and the governments they represented, he was invulnerable.

The Lord Jesus takes the soul of the sinner who believes in Him and covers the guilty one with His blood. Thus wrapped and sheltered by the Savior, he is safe.

David Jeremiah

GOD'S TRAINING PROCESS

He who is faithful in what is least is faithful also in much.
LUKE 16:10

Joseph was cooperative with God's process of training. Joseph had to go through thirteen years of schooling so that he could experience eighty years of ministry. Throughout all that training, Joseph focused on the Lord. In slavery, in the pit, and in prison, he worked to become a strong, disciplined man of God. There was no complaining, simply a desire to obey the Lord and do his best.

If we are God's people, we will be obedient to Him no matter what our situation. Joseph was faithful in every circumstance, and the Lord blessed him. He proved himself faithful in a home, and God put him in charge of a prison. He proved himself faithful in a prison, and God put him in charge of a nation. God used Joseph because he was cooperative with God's training process, and the Lord is still looking for cooperative men and women today.

A HUNGER FOR GOD

O God, You are my God; . . . my soul thirsts for You; my flesh longs for You.
PSALM 63:1

It is amazing that with no knowledge of eternal life, no knowledge of a sacrificial Savior, no knowledge of the resurrection—all the things we know well in the New Testament era—Old Testament saints like David had such a longing for God. They had a sense of His presence with them that few Christians seem to enjoy in our day.

David must have already learned that even the royal trappings of kingship could not provide what his heart needed, that only God could slake his thirst and satisfy his longing. He had lived long enough to know that none of what the world offers, whether in the desert or the palace, could satisfy the longings of his heart.

Someone has said that Satan knows nothing of true pleasure and satisfaction, that he is an expert only in amusements. David had learned the difference, and we would do well to imitate him. True pleasure comes from knowing God, being known by God, and being at rest in His presence.

David Jeremiah

GOD FORGIVES

If we confess our sins, He is faithful and just to forgive us our sins and to cleanse us from all unrighteousness.

1 JOHN 1:9

What happens when we fail? What happens when we do not take God up on His promise? Reading this verse in view of the faithfulness of God puts it in a whole new light. We may feel our sin is too bad to be forgiven. But this scripture says that when we confess, God forgives. If you refuse to believe that, it's an affront to the faithfulness of God who cannot and will not and shall not lie. God says if we confess it, He will cleanse it. And He risks His faithfulness on that promise.

When asked, "What does the faithfulness of God make you think of first?" many people reply that it makes them think of their own unfaithfulness and the way they fail Him. But Scripture goes on record as saying that, even when we fail, God does not. "If we are faithless, He remains faithful; He cannot deny Himself" (2 Timothy 2:13).

You can say you don't deserve the faithfulness of God. None of us does. That isn't the issue. The issue is that even when we are faithless, He is faithful.

DISCOVER GOD'S WORK
FOR YOU

We are His workmanship, created in Christ Jesus for good works, which God prepared beforehand that we should walk in them.

EPHESIANS 2:10

So often in the past I have concentrated on this goal and that goal. I'm really into goals, objectives, and plans—both in my personal life and as the pastor of a church. But I believe that people should not concentrate so much on the goal as on the power. And as we pray, we may discover that what we thought were great and lofty goals are pale and puny alongside His goals for our life and ministry.

Let us ask God to make us faithful as people of prayer, and let us pray that God will do His work through us. Then, whatever God wants to do, let's be open to it!

I have no idea what God is up to in your life and mine, but as He works through His mighty Spirit, we are about to find out! I promise you, it will not be on anybody's chart. You are not going to find a framed copy of it hanging on the wall of some office. God is going to do it in His own way—in startling, unexpected ways—through us as we trust Him and as we pray.

David Jeremiah

BLIND HOPE

By faith Abraham obeyed when he was called to go out to the place which he would receive as an inheritance. And he went out, not knowing where he was going.

HEBREWS 11:8

Hope is necessary in our lives today because often the way is unknown. God came to Abraham and said, "I want you to go to a place that I have charted out for you. I want you to leave your home and your family and go there." He didn't give Abraham a map. He just said, "Go," and Abraham pulled up everything and he left.

God came to Abraham and said, "I am going to bless you with a son, and out of that son is going to be a nation. In fact, you are going to have so many descendants that they will be like the sands of the sea and the stars of the sky because you won't be able to number them. I'm going to bless you, and I'm going to bless your son, and I'm going to bless the whole nation that comes from this promise."

What a wonderful promise—except that when Abraham got those words he was already in his nineties and didn't have a son. It was the hope that Abraham had in his heart that helped him get through the way he didn't know. Abraham woke up every morning not knowing what God was up to, but his hope helped him hold on to what God had told him.

YOU CAN'T KNOW ALL GOD'S SECRETS

The secret things belong to the LORD our God.

DEUTERONOMY 29:29

We would be less than honest if we denied the tension that exists between God's sovereignty and man's responsibility. God is in control, but man is responsible. An old Puritan preacher had a wise perspective on the dilemma. He said that he just preached both God's sovereignty and man's responsibility as hard as he could. In Luke 22:22, Jesus said, "And truly the Son of Man goes as it has been determined, but woe to that man by whom He is betrayed!" Do you see both parts of the tension in this verse? It was determined by God that Jesus should be betrayed—but "woe to that man" who does the betraying.

A key verse in all these matters is Deuteronomy 29:29: "The secret things belong to the Lord our God, but those things which are revealed belong to us and to our children forever, that we may do all the words of this law." The secret things are God's determined, sovereign purpose. Our problem is wanting to know all God's secrets. But our responsibility is to take what God has revealed and work to understand it and implement it with all our heart—and leave everything else to God.

David Jeremiah

OUR GIGANTIC SECRET

*These things I have spoken to you, that My joy may remain in you,
and that your joy may be full.*

JOHN 15:11

The Bible shows that joy is present in all of the major events of the Christian life. There is joy in salvation, in baptism, when we read the Word of God, and in prayer. In fact, Christian joy is so unique that the Bible teaches us that it comes even at times of discouragement—even when we are dying.

G. K. Chesterton wrote that "joy is the gigantic secret of the Christian." I believe he's right. This kind of joy is not known anyplace else in the world except in the life of a person who knows Jesus Christ in a personal way.

Jesus said, "These things I have spoken to you, that My joy may remain in you, and that your joy may be full" (John 15:11). The center of joy for the Christian is Christ. The joy is Christ's joy. It is simply the life of the Lord Jesus Christ being lived out in an individual. Christian joy is letting Christ live His life out through you so that you become what He is. There are other kinds of joy found in other places in the world, but there is no place where you can find Christian joy except in Christ.

THE GREAT DIVIDE

Between us and you there is a great gulf fixed, so that those who want to pass from here to you cannot, nor can those from there pass to us.

LUKE 16:26

The gulf between Hades and Paradise is fixed—immovable. The gulf is not going to be taken away. What you do in this life fixes forever where you will spend eternity. If you reject Jesus Christ in this life, you will remain in hell forever. There is no crossing back, no second chance, no coming back and starting over.

Thankfully, the decision you make for Jesus Christ in this life fixes your eternal salvation forever as well. The point is that the gulf, the divide between heaven and hell, is a fixed divide. Therefore, whatever decision you make in this life—for or against Jesus Christ—is a decision that you will live with for eternity. No one knows what the next minute, hour, day, or year will bring. The decision you die with is the decision you will live with forever.

David Jeremiah

MEDITATE ON THE LORD

I remember You on my bed, I meditate on You in the night watches.
PSALM 63:6

Many people spend their nights tossing and turning when they face difficult circumstances. But not David. When he lay on his bed at night, he simply meditated on the Lord. He remembered the many ways in which God had been faithful to him in the past.

Are you losing sleep over a situation or circumstance in your life? As you think about the past, the present, and the future, meditate upon it from God's perspective. Keeping hope alive is partly based on reliving the memories of the good things we have experienced as a child of God and the difficult things God brought us through.

Think of what David must have meditated upon. David stood before that mountain of a man with three things: a sling, a bag of stones, and faith in the power of God to give him victory. And that was all he needed—the battle was his. Never forget what God has done for you in the past. Those victories will fuel your faith in victories yet to come.

DECIDE TO LOVE

This is My commandment, that you love one another as I have loved you.
JOHN 15:12

A*gape* love is God's special kind of self-giving. *Agape* describes a love that comes from and is rooted in God. It is totally selfless love. It delights in giving, even though the loved one may be unkind, unlovely, and unworthy. *Agape* love continues to give.

Agape determines to do whatever is best for the loved one. It willingly sacrifices itself for another's good. *Agape* gives when it gets nothing in return. It does not even think of getting something back.

Do you think love is just a feeling? It is not a feeling. Love is a decision. The Bible says God is love. God is not a feeling. The Bible says we are commanded to love. We don't have any option.

Maybe you don't feel like loving. Do it anyway. God commands you to love. Maybe you think you can't love. Then find out whatever it is you are supposed to do when you love somebody and do all those things. Depend upon God to do His part. When we do what we're commanded in obedience to God, we discover that grace begins to develop in our lives.

David Jeremiah

TO KNOW THE LORD, WAIT

I wait for the LORD, my soul waits, and in His word I do hope.
PSALM 130:5

There is a sense in which we have to wait before God for Him to reveal Himself to us so we can learn more about Him. The reason has to do with how we learn anything. We learn things in the human realm by acquiring a new piece of knowledge and comparing it to something we already know. But with God, since He is beyond our finding out, we have nothing to compare Him to.

We can never know God completely because we don't have enough common ground to associate who He is with what we know. And so we are consigned to waiting before Him as He reveals more of Himself to us. If that seems strange to us, it is because we are not used to thinking of God in the truly transcendent terms in which He exists. As we grow in our experience and knowledge of God, we develop more and more common ground with Him by which we can learn even more. Therefore, knowing God is a process, and waiting before Him in worship is the means to knowing Him better.

YIELD TO GOD

He who calls you is faithful, who also will do it.

1 THESSALONIANS 5:24

Pastors and ministers struggle with the temptation to get "stressed out" as much as any other Christian. Sometimes I can let the expectations of the members of my church become so many separate circles of responsibility that I begin to be stressed about meeting all those expectations. Pastors are expected to visit everyone who goes to the hospital, counsel everyone who has a problem, go to see every new visitor, and preach dynamic messages three or four times each week. Any pastor who tries to do all those things will find himself burned out in a matter of weeks, months, or years—and many have.

The only way I survive as a pastor of a large church is to know that the very best thing I can do for our church is to do the will of God. God loves each person in our church, and I know if I am following His plan and will for me, the congregation's needs will be met. I constantly have to bring myself back under His authority and learn from Him how to stay focused on His will for my life.

David Jeremiah

SEEK TO SERVE OUR REDEEMER

Having been set free from sin, you became slaves of righteousness.
ROMANS 6:18

As familiar as many of us are with the Passover and Exodus, one aspect of that great event is often overlooked: God redeemed His chosen people from bondage to Pharaoh for the purpose that they might become slaves to Him. Freedom for the sake of absolute freedom from all responsibility was never God's purpose. The children of Israel, once they came out of Egypt, did not suddenly scatter to the four points of the compass to do whatever they wished. God's desire was that they might walk in His will and invest their freedom from bondage in obedience to His will. Why? So He might bless them! When they failed to obey Him, He did not revoke their redemption and send them back into bondage—but they did miss out on the temporal blessings of continued obedience.

The parallel between the nation of Israel in the Old Testament and the individual believer today is inescapable. We should invest our freedom from slavery to sin, not in indulging the whims of the flesh, but in seeking to serve the God who redeemed us.

TRANSFORMATION POWER

I was formerly a blasphemer, a persecutor, and an insolent man;
but I obtained mercy.

1 TIMOTHY 1:13

The great glory of the story of the apostle Paul is knowing what he had been before seeing what he became. The greatest enemy of the Lord Jesus Christ in the first century became His greatest servant, most trusted apostle, and a faithful friend. The same hand that wrote out indictments of heresy against the early church was the hand that wrote the letters upon which the early church was based and ultimately spread. The heart that rejoiced when Stephen was stoned to death became a heart that rejoiced at the privilege of suffering for Christ's sake. The noble statements of theology in Romans, the sweet lyrics of Christian love in 1 Corinthians 13, and the desire to reach the regions beyond with the gospel all came from the former persecutor of Christ and His church.

If ever there was any evidence of the transforming power of the gospel, it is seen in the life of Saul the persecutor who became Paul the apostle. Hopefully that same gospel has transformed you as well. If so, like Paul, may you ask the Lord today, "What do You want me to do?"

David Jeremiah

CHRIST'S COMMUNICATION

These are written that you may believe Jesus is the Christ, the Son of God, and that believing you may have life in His name.

JOHN 20:31

Jesus was not only victorious over death, but He reached out to all those around Him. He desperately wanted to communicate with those who had been closest to Him. He used His scars with Thomas, His voice with Mary, the breaking of bread with two disciples, and a repeated fishing adventure with the other disciples because He loved them and wanted to reveal Himself to them.

He still has that passion today. We are so blessed to have the precious Word of God, the record of all the Lord did to reveal Himself to people. By it He has communicated to us, asking us to believe so that we may have life.

He continues to reach out to people today, through His church, through radio and television messages, through books and tapes, and through the personal witness of those who know Him as their personal Savior. He keeps on reaching to us with the message that He is alive, and because He lives, we may live also.

TRUST IN THE GIVER,
NOT THE GIFTS

He who trusts in his riches will fall, but the righteous will flourish like foliage.

PROVERBS 11:28

Proverbs' primary principle on the governance of money is found in 11:28: "He who trusts in his riches will fall, but the righteous will flourish like foliage."

There is nothing wrong with obtaining riches, but there is a great deal wrong with trusting in them instead of trusting in the One who gives them—and who can take them away. We are warned against greed and against putting our trust in transitory things like wealth so that nothing comes between us and God.

Money is not given to us as a permanent possession, and therefore should never be the object of trust. God, on the other hand, is permanent and eternal, the perfect object for our trust. Therefore, we are to trust the Giver, not the gift, when it comes to material prosperity.

If we manage what God has given, we will have enough money to give away.

David Jeremiah

GOD'S BEAUTIFUL CREATION

The earth is full of the goodness of the LORD.

PSALM 33:5

God loves to bring about blessings in our lives. We can see the goodness of God not only by how He provides for us in our own lives, but also by looking at the beauty that He built into the universe He created. The psalmist says, "The earth is full of the goodness of the Lord." Arthur W. Pink writes that the goodness of God is seen in the variety of natural pleasures that He has provided for us. God could have satisfied our hunger without worrying about our taste, but He gives us taste buds and gratifies them with good-tasting food. God could have made the earth fertile without its surface being so delightfully beautiful. We could have lived without beautiful flowers and the music of birds. But the source of all this loveliness and charm leads us back to the goodness of God.

We have a beautiful world, and every time we have a chance to visit the greatness and goodness of God in His provision of this beauty for us, we ought to stop and praise His name. He has cared so wonderfully for us as His creatures.

OVERCOMING PEER PRESSURE

Do not be deceived: "Evil company corrupts good habits."

1 CORINTHIANS 15:33

One of my favorite television shows over the years has been *Candid Camera*. I especially enjoyed the segments when the situations illustrated peer pressure. In one sketch, there was an elevator full of actors all facing the back of the elevator. When the doors opened and the unsuspecting "guinea pig" stepped in, he was the only one facing the correct way. But eventually the camera showed him turning around the wrong way as well. He couldn't take the pressure of being the only one doing the right thing.

The pressure to conform is at its very greatest during the years when a young person is moving from childhood to adulthood. During that time in our lives we want to be accepted so badly that we are very vulnerable to group pressure. And don't think this pressure doesn't impact Christian young people. Whether it's drugs being passed around a car, a party where alcohol is available, or a slumber party where sexual exploits are discussed, there is immense pressure on young people to conform to society's standards. Peer pressure among young people today is one of the strongest forces for ruining lives. And it's time we as parents and young people get on top of the problem and begin to develop a strategy to overcome it.

David Jeremiah

PRAY AT ALL TIMES

He spoke a parable to them, that men always ought to pray and not lose heart.
LUKE 18:1

Here is something I have learned about prayer that I have not seen mentioned in books on prayer I have read: prayer is meant to be preventative more than remedial. We usually treat prayer as remedial, meaning we pray when we have a need or are in trouble. But in Luke 18:1, Jesus says that at all times we "ought to pray . . . and not lose heart." In other words, prayer isn't the last thought; it's the first thought. It is preventative, not remedial. Also instead of praying when we are tempted, Jesus says we should pray that we may not "enter into temptation" (Matthew 26:41). When we are not under pressure and stress, we should be praying so that we might be shored up and defended against the pressures that will come.

Until we come to the place of prayer, we will never find release from stress. If we treat prayer as just a religious ritual or option, then we are not truly living in dependence upon God. Prayer is the soul of man crying out in inadequacy to a God who is adequate, a God who is able to do what man cannot.

DIVINE DIRECTION

May the Lord direct your hearts into the love of God and into the patience of Christ.

2 THESSALONIANS 3:5

The nineteenth century was the period of westward expansion as wagon trains rolled across the Great Plains toward California. By the 1850s, some of the most sought-after people in America were the frontier scouts. Men like Kit Carson and Jim Bridger, who had spent years exploring the western regions, were hired to lead the pioneers safely to their destination. They alone knew the dangers and how to avoid them. They couldn't move the Rocky Mountains, but they knew the way through them.

When the apostle Paul prayed that God would "direct" believers, he was praying that God would go before them and remove the obstacles in their way—the literal meaning of the word *direct*. God doesn't just point and say, "Go there." Like a frontier scout, He leads the way and removes the obstacles and dangers that would keep us from growing in maturity in Christ. But be careful if you pray Paul's prayer! What you count as a possession—a relationship, a material idol, a secret sin—God may see as a problem and remove it.

Life is filled with obstacles to maturity. Only God can remove them, helping us grow up before we grow old.

David Jeremiah

SPEAK SOFTLY

A soft answer turns away wrath, but a harsh word stirs up anger.

PROVERBS 15:1

The mouth of the righteous is a well of life (Proverbs 10:11) and is as valuable as silver (v. 20). The words of the righteous are wisdom; they are like food for those hungry to know how to live (vv. 21, 31). And most of all, the lips of the righteous are discerning, knowing what is acceptable to say (v. 32). I believe the sensitive, Spirit-led Christian can depend upon the Holy Spirit to give him freedom to speak or freedom not to speak, depending on whether the words are appropriate in the given situation.

Perhaps the most underutilized word of healing that Proverbs discusses is the "soft answer [that] turns away wrath." It takes two people to have a heated, angry argument. If one of them decides to use a soft answer and not participate in the shouting match, the heated argument must, by definition, come to a halt. If you enter a situation where an angry argument is taking place, you can diffuse the tension and lower the decibel level by your soft words.

It is a blessing beyond description to see the spirits of a person rise, the life restored to their eyes, as a result of a healing word from your own lips.

ROBIN HOOD AND LITTLE JOHN

If when we were enemies we were reconciled to God through the death of His Son, much more, having been reconciled, we shall be saved by His life.

ROMANS 5:10

Anyone who knows the story of Robin Hood will recall the first time the celebrated thief encountered Little John. Both men were traveling through the forest heading toward each other. They first saw each other at the opposite ends of a bridge that was designed to hold just one man at a time. Each was too proud to let the other pass first, so they both started across. They met at the middle, exchanged insults, and began to fight. As the story goes, both men fell into the waters below. Later, as they recovered on the banks of the river, they began to laugh at themselves. Subsequently, they became the best of friends. Not only had these adversaries settled their differences; they had gone a step further, becoming good friends.

Before we became Christians, we were in effect opposed to God. Our surrender to him didn't lead to a mere master-slave relationship. As Paul says, Jesus Christ's act of love has made His friends.

David Jeremiah

THE UNTAMED TONGUE

Every kind of beast and bird, of reptile and creature of the sea, is tamed and has been tamed by mankind. But no man can tame the tongue.

JAMES 3:7–8

James says we are able to control every kind of beast and animal, yet we have not learned how to control the tongue. After God created man, he was to rule over the fish, birds, cattle, and every creeping thing (Genesis 1:26). When Noah came out of the ark, God reiterated His purpose: "And the fear of you and the dread of you shall be on every beast of the earth, on every bird of the air, on all that move on the earth, and on all the fish of the sea. They are given into your hand" (9:2).

Today, the nature of the animal has been tamed by the nature of man. We have dancing bears, trained seals, talking dolphins, acrobatic birds, charmed snakes, dogs jumping through hoops, and lions with their mouths open wide and the trainer's head inside. We have elephants that march in line behind one another with riders perched on top. All of these creatures have been tamed, but the tongue is untamed and untamable without God's help.

IN-YOUR-FACE FOREVER FRIENDS

As iron sharpens iron, so a man sharpens the countenance of his friend.

PROVERBS 27:17

Proverbs 27:17 suggests, "As iron sharpens iron, so a man sharpens the countenance of his friend." An in-your-face friend is one who will tackle the tough issues of life with you—someone who is not offended if you disagree with him and someone who is not afraid to disagree with you. You both have higher goals than agreement.

Proverbs 17:17 says, "A friend loves at all times, and a brother is born for adversity." The best way to determine who your "forever friends" are is to go through a crisis. Adversity is like a filter—it separates those who are loyal from those who are not. You cannot tell your true friends until adversity appears. Your friends may not even know whether they are loyal friends until they are asked to identify with your suffering. It is easy to be a friend when things are good and pleasant. But the number of people who will stand beside you decreases as the temperature of your crisis goes up.

How does one get that kind of friend? By being one. Proverbs 18:24 says, "A man who has friends must himself be friendly." How many times have you proven yourself to be a forever friend by sticking close to someone through their time of trouble and adversity?

David Jeremiah

SEPTEMBER

My God shall supply all your need according to His riches in glory by Christ Jesus.

—PHILIPPIANS 4:19

A PATTERN OF LIFE

I will bless the LORD at all times; His praise shall continually be in my mouth.

PSALM 34:1

It has been said that too many Christians worship their work, work at their play, and play at their worship. What we do on Sundays we call "worship," but is it really? For many people the subject of worship is an enigma. They come to services and sing, but they sense something is missing. They pray and talk with God each day, but find themselves wondering if perhaps there is something they failed to learn about their life with God.

When you begin to read the Scriptures and study the people of the Old Testament, you cannot read far before you begin to understand that worship was the pattern of their lives. The Lord Himself designed the first worship center. He was very specific; it took seven chapters to describe how He wanted it built. He made it portable and designed it to be a visual aid for the worshiping Israelites. The tabernacle was the center of the encampment of God's people. It was a way of showing that God was to be at the center of His people in worship as a way of life. Worship is at the top of God's priority list.

EMPTYING THE NEST

Therefore a man shall leave his father and mother and be joined to his wife, and they shall become one flesh.

GENESIS 2:24

As our kids become older, we notice that, little by little, we are losing control. That's what parenting is all about: the gradual loss of control. That's when we find out how well we've done.

Ultimately all of us must say good-bye to our kids. Yet sometimes I find myself thinking angry thoughts about the process of emptying the nest. It just doesn't seem fair to invest twenty prime years—the best years of my life—in four kids, only to see them walk away one by one and leave me for their own lives.

Whose idea was this anyway?

Let me answer that question from Genesis 2:24: "Therefore a man shall leave his father and mother and be joined to his wife, and they shall become one flesh." The Bible makes it clear that this whole leaving thing was God's idea. As sad as we sometimes feel, as much as we grieve, as often as dread creeps into our lives when our kids move into their high school years, we need to remember this: the empty nest was God's idea.

PROMISES AND PREDICTIONS

Look up and lift up your heads, because your redemption draws near.

LUKE 21:28

In 1949, the magazine *Popular Science* predicted, "Computers in the future may weigh no more than 1.5 tons." In 1977, Ken Olsen, founder of Digital Equipment Corporation, said, "There is no reason anyone would want a computer in their home." Bill Gates said in 1981, "640K ought to be enough for anybody."

Making predictions is risky business—unless you are God! According to John Wesley White, the coming again of Christ and the end of the age occupies some 1,845 scriptural verses, and each one offers sure and certain hope for the Christian. Just consider these promises: "For the Lord Himself will descend from heaven with a shout, with the voice of an archangel, and with the trumpet of God. And the dead in Christ will rise first" (1 Thessalonians 4:16). "I will come again and receive you to Myself; that where I am, there you may be also" (John 14:3). "Behold, I am coming quickly!"(Revelation 22:7).

Vance Havner said, "We are not just looking for something to happen; we are looking for Someone to come! And when these things begin to come to pass, we are not to drop our heads in discouragement or shake our heads in despair, but rather lift up our heads in delight."

David Jeremiah

CLING TO GOD

The salvation of the righteous is from the LORD; He is their strength in the time of trouble.

PSALM 37:39

Here's a way for you to think about this the next time trouble comes: if you and God are standing apart from one another, and trouble comes between you, it can drive you further apart. But when you see trouble coming and cling to God with all your might, you never let trouble come between you and God—then you have the victory. In fact, the pressure of the trouble will push you closer and closer to God. It will only serve to strengthen your relationship with Him. People tell me all the time, and I can testify as well, that they never experience the nearness of God as much as they do when they are in the desert places of life. That happens by not letting trouble come between you and God.

Prayer is a way to cling to God. You reach out to Him and communicate with Him with the words of your heart. You pour out your praises and your petitions, and you stay in an attitude of prayer until deliverance comes.

A LIVING EXAMPLE

The things which you learned and received and heard and saw in me, these do, and the God of peace will be with you.

PHILIPPIANS 4:9

The Philippian believers were instructed to practice the things they had heard, seen, learned, and received from Paul. The items on that action list included:

- Loving more
- Having greater discernment
- Being sincere and without offense
- Being filled with the fruits of righteousness
- Having conduct worthy of the gospel
- Standing fast in one spirit
- Striving together for the gospel
- Being like-minded, of one accord
- Esteeming others better than themselves
- Working out their own salvation in fear and trembling
- Doing all things without complaining and disputing
- Holding fast the Word of Life
- Looking out for false teachers

When Paul spoke of the things learned and received, he was talking about careful exhortation. When he spoke of those things heard and seen, he was referring to concrete example. Paul was a living example of the conduct he expected from the Philippians.

David Jeremiah

HOW TO BUILD UP OTHERS

Encourage one another and build each other up, just as in fact you are doing.

1 THESSALONIANS 5:11 NIV

We say, "I'm going to sit down and figure out how I can build others up." That's fine, but how do we build others up? How do we know what to do?

Paul gave this advice in Acts 20:32: "So now, brethren, I commend you to God and to the word of His grace, which is able to build you up and give you an inheritance among all those who are sanctified."

How do we get built up enough to build up somebody else? My friends, it's the Bible. Read the Bible. The Word of God is the fuel to help us be builders. In 1 Peter 2:2, we are told, "As newborn babes, desire the pure milk of the word, that you may grow thereby."

One New Testament passage, Jude 1:20–21, talks about building ourselves up: "But you, beloved, building yourselves up on your most holy faith, praying in the Holy Spirit, keep yourselves in the love of God, looking for the mercy of our Lord Jesus Christ unto eternal life."

What does Jesus want us to do? I think He wants us to be builders—edifiers—men and women who are committed to strengthening the body. Let us build one another up!

THE POISON OF GOSSIP

He who covers a transgression seeks love, but he who repeats a matter separates friends.

PROVERBS 17:9

For many Christians, the indoor sport of choice is gossip. Only we don't call it gossip—we say we are "sharing prayer requests." The book of Proverbs speaks volumes about the poison that can be spread by the tongue: "He who repeats a matter separates friends" (17:9; see also 16:27–28; 18:8; 26:18–22).

A story is told of a woman who learned this lesson the hard way. She gossiped extensively about another woman, only to discover that all she had been repeating was not true. She sought the advice of her pastor on how to make things right. He told her to take a feather pillow, cut a hole in it, and go around town sprinkling the feathers everywhere she went.

The next day, he told her to go back through town and collect each of the tiny feathers. The woman realized that she could no more retract the damage done by her words than she could collect thousands of tiny feathers scattered by the wind.

David Jeremiah

KEEP BUILDING THE CHURCH

Each of us should please his neighbor for his good, to build him up.

ROMANS 15:2 NIV

I will never forget the process of building the worship center for our church. It was exciting, a vision taking shape before our eyes. Even now I can visualize every step of the process: from the time the backhoe dug the first scoop of dirt until the carpet was laid in the finished building.

We get excited about buildings and seeing them take shape. However, the New Testament is much more concerned about building people. Build up the body of Christ. That, I believe, is what you and I are to be about as the last days come upon us.

With all my heart, I want every year of my life to be a building year. I'm not speaking of physical buildings, though some may be built. I'm referring to the building of God's people. I want to build up the body of Christ until He comes or calls me home. Join me, please.

THE WORDS OF GOD

That which was from the beginning, which we have heard, which we have seen with our eyes, which we have looked at and our hands have touched—this we proclaim concerning the Word of life.

1 JOHN 1:1 NIV

It was the ancient Greeks who first sent representatives to conduct official business on behalf of their government. Today, ambassadors speak with the full authority of their governments, and embassies are considered inviolable territory. In short, how a nation treats another nation's ambassador and embassy is a good indication of the esteem in which it holds the foreign nation as a whole.

The idea of identifying and valuing two entities as equals is a biblical concept. For two people in covenant, to harm one was to harm the other (1 Samuel 18:1–4). And to disregard a person's word was to disparage the person himself (Luke 6:46). Therefore, how we value the Living Word of God, Jesus Christ, is a good indicator of how we value the written Word of God, the Bible. What conclusions would someone draw about your love for the Savior after observing your relationship to the Scriptures for a few weeks? Since both the Bible and Jesus Christ are the Word of God, it's impossible to value one and not the other.

A proven way to grow closer to God is to grow closer to God's Word.

David Jeremiah

WHAT, LORD?

Our hope for you is steadfast, because we know that as you are partakers of the sufferings, so also you will partake of the consolation.

2 CORINTHIANS 1:7

During stormy weather, when the strong winds blow, the roots of plants actually dig down deeper. Then when the calm days return, the new roots provide a deeper foundation for new growth. That is the way it should be with us. What we receive from disruptive moments depends upon how we respond.

The right question is never, "Why, Lord?" It is always, "What, Lord? What do You want to teach me through this disruptive moment? Take me around and through the bend in the road as my Teacher. Don't let me miss anything that You want me to see and learn."

Dear friend, if you face a disruptive moment with any other perspective than that, it will just be a bump in the road that bounces you all over the highway. When it is over you will just be sore, and you won't be any better. Purpose now, before you get to the bends in the road, that you will respond in a way that produces more of God's will in your life.

THE OUTCOME IS CONFIRMED

Thanks be to God, who gives us the victory through our Lord Jesus Christ.

1 CORINTHIANS 15:57

On Tuesday, September 11, 2001, the United States of America was attacked by hostile forces. The destruction wrought by terrorists in New York City and Washington, D.C. was the first time anyone in modern times had brought so serious an attack within the continental boundaries of America.

The US president George W. Bush interpreted the attacks as acts of war and immediately declared war on terrorism. The declaration itself is evidence of the changing face of warfare in the modern era. For the first time, war is being declared by America not on an offending nation, but on an ideology—the ideology of terrorism. Compared to warfare strategies of the past, this is a new direction—but one wrought out of necessity.

The weapons of war are new. Diplomatic strategies, embargoes, financial tools, trade and social strategies will be used to isolate and ostracize nations in the world community that do not eagerly join the worldwide fight against terrorism. Finally, military will be employed.

Unlike military conflicts in this world, the outcome of our spiritual warfare is already confirmed: Satan will be defeated and believers in Jesus Christ will reign triumphantly with Him forever.

VICTORIOUS WARRIORS

*Whatever is born of God overcomes the world. And this is the victory
that has overcome the world—our faith.*

1 JOHN 5:4

The Bible says that Satan's purpose is to blind sinners and beguile Christians, and to hurt and discourage those who belong to God. He will do anything to disturb the mind, deceive the heart, and defeat life. He is actively involved in the world today, and if you read your Bible, you'll find he has always been active: he led Lot into Sodom, got Peter to deny Christ, made Ananias and Sapphira lie to the church, and even dared attack Jesus Christ. If he isn't afraid to attack the Lord of glory, you should not be surprised to discover that he is willing to attack the most mature Christian. He wants to bring division into the church today, paralyzing its ministry and scandalizing its leaders.

Yet the Word of God tells us that this warfare is one for which we can prepare. We can walk into a hostile environment and do warfare for God and not be defeated. Our Commander in Chief has already won the war, and He is waiting for us to get in on the victory. God can help us to learn how to be victorious warriors in the great spiritual battle.

TRUST GOD TO FULFILL
YOUR NEEDS

My God shall supply all your need according to His riches in glory by Christ Jesus.
PHILIPPIANS 4:19

Paul reminded the Philippians that the God who had cared for *his* needs through their loving concern would also care for *their* needs as they trusted Him! This promise is often taken out of context. It was given to encourage those who were sacrificial in response to the needs of God's work. There is another promise very similar to this one that is also found in the middle of some strong teaching on steward-ship: "And God is able to make all grace abound toward you, that you, always having all sufficiency in all things, may have an abundance for every good work" (2 Corinthians 9:8).

Paul had been rejoicing in the fact that the Philippians had supplied his need. Now he told them that God would supply their need. His promise to them was *personal*: "my God." It was *positive*: "shall supply." It was *pointed*: "all your need." It was *plentiful*: "according to His riches in glory." And it was *powerful*: "by Christ Jesus."

This is a consistent principle in the working of God with men. "Give, and it will be given to you: good measure, pressed down, shaken together, and running over will be put into your bosom. For with the same measure that you use, it will be measured back to you" (Luke 6:38).

David Jeremiah

REFRESHING FRIENDS

Ointment and perfume delight the heart, and the sweetness of a man's friend gives delight by hearty counsel.

PROVERBS 27:9

P roverbs 27:9 says that "hearty counsel," or the kind of advice that comes from a good friend, is as pleasant as "ointment and perfume." Good, strong advice from a good, strong friend is a delight to receive. It shows that a person really cares about you and wants your best. "Hearty counsel" builds you up and strengthens you and helps you face difficult things.

These words, attributed to George Eliot, define a fortifying friend: "Oh, the inexpressible comfort of feeling safe with a person, having neither to weigh thoughts nor measure words, but pouring them all right out, just as they are, chaff and grain together, certain that a faithful hand will take and sift them, keep what is worth keeping, and then, with the breath of kindness, blow the rest away."

The Bible contains a wonderful example of a fortifying friendship between two men, David and Jonathan. In spite of circumstances that would make their friendship an unlikely one, they forged a bond that fortified each of them. Their relationship stands as a testament to what true friendship can endure and accomplish.

PRAYER ATTACK

Continue earnestly in prayer, being vigilant in it with thanksgiving.

COLOSSIANS 4:2

During World War I, the French decided to take one of the enemy's strategic strongholds. But the enemy's lines were so defended by trenches, parapets, and barbed wire that it was virtually impossible for the infantry to get through.

But the attacking general had amassed a large amount of powerful artillery. He began to fire round after round of the most explosive shells at them. With this excessive strength, a continuous fire was kept up for more than five hours, until all the trenches were covered, palisades thrown down, and wire entanglements blown to pieces. The infantry was then able to enter and capture the base with ease.

This incident is analogous to spiritual warfare. There are positions of the adversary that cannot be stormed or starved. There are defenses that seem impregnable. But with a barrage of constant prayer, the defenses can be lowered, and souls will be ready to surrender to the Lord. Let us be productive soldiers in the battle against sin and Satan.

David Jeremiah

NOW IS THE TIME TO OBEY

You do not know what will happen tomorrow. For what is your life? It is even a vapor that appears for a little time and then vanishes away.

JAMES 4:14

We discover from the Old Testament that the destructive practice of procrastination has been around for a long time (Proverbs 3:27–28; Isaiah 56:12). But the Bible has written the word *NOW* in large letters in the gospel message. "Behold, now is the accepted time; behold, now is the day of salvation" (2 Corinthians 6:2). The time for obedience is now! We cannot count on tomorrow, so we must take advantage of today. In business terms, yesterday is a canceled check. Tomorrow is a promissory note. Today is the only cash you have.

According to James, knowledge and responsibility work together. To sin ignorantly is one thing, but to sin in the face of known truth is quite another. Statements from our Lord and the apostle Peter confirm the truth that James presents in verse 17: We are held accountable for what we know but fail (or choose not) to do (Luke 12:47–48; 2 Peter 2:21). Sins of omission are just as serious as sins of commission. To omit God from the planning processes of our lives, knowing that we should include Him, is sin.

JESUS: MAN OF HIS WORD

Let not your heart be troubled; you believe in God, believe also in Me.

JOHN 14:1

A young boy was out in the country, climbing among a row of cliffs. He yelled from the top of one, "Hey, Dad! Catch me!" The father turned around to see his son joyfully jumping off a rock straight at him. The dad became an instant circus act, catching his son, causing them both to fall to the ground.

When the father found his voice, he gasped in exasperation, "Son, can you give me one good reason why you did that?" He responded with remarkable calmness: "Sure . . . because you're my dad." His whole assurance was based on the fact that his father was trustworthy.

As Christians, we can throw ourselves into the arms of Jesus because He is trustworthy. We can stake our lives upon His promises because He is a Man of His Word. If doubts assail us, we must simply look at the convincing evidence—His perfect track record! For instance, He said He would die and He did (Matthew 20:18). He said He would rise from the dead on the third day and He did (v. 19). He said He would return to His Father and He did (John 7:33).

Because Jesus is a Man of His Word, we can be assured He will keep His future promises as well. He said He will return for us and He will (14:3).

David Jeremiah

HIS WONDERFUL PRESENCE

You shall worship the LORD your God, and Him only you shall serve.
MATTHEW 4:10

God exists everywhere, but He is not always manifest everywhere. His manifest presence comes to us when He is praised. C. S. Lewis once wrote that "it is in the process of being worshiped that God communicates His presence to men . . . even in Judaism the essence of the sacrifice was not really that men gave bulls and goats to God, but that by their so doing God gave Himself to men."

Perhaps you have experienced the wonderful presence of God during a special time of worship. As you were singing, praying, praising, and worshiping the Lord, you felt His presence closer to you than ever before! Worship causes the presence of God to be felt and experienced by His people. If you really want God to be in your church meetings, praise Him as best you can.

Satan tempted Jesus by asking for His worship, not His service: "All these things I will give You if You will fall down and worship me" (Matthew 4:9). Satan understands the correct order—the one you worship is the one you will serve. And keep in mind Christ's response in verse 10: "You shall worship the Lord your God, and Him only you shall serve."

THE POWER OF THE WORD

*For the word of God is living and powerful, and sharper than any
two-edged sword.*

HEBREWS 4:12

A young German monk desperately wanted to find
relief for his tormented soul. He prayed, studied, and
even went on a pilgrimage to Rome, but he still found no
peace. Finally, when studying Paul's letter to the Romans,
the eyes of his heart were opened: "The righteous will live
by faith" (Romans 1:17 NIV). Martin Luther, the father of the
Protestant Reformation, finally found the assurance he had
sought for so long.

Because the Word of God is alive (Hebrews 4:12), it is
able to bring about changes of all sorts. Whereas Martin
Luther was able to find assurance of salvation through
faith alone, another person may find freedom from anxiety
through knowledge of God's sovereign control over life. The
Word of God is used by the Holy Spirit to probe the deepest
parts of the human heart and bring illumination. Perhaps
there is an area of life where change has eluded you. If you
will search the Word of God, you will discover the truth the
Holy Spirit can use to satisfy your deepest longing (Proverbs
2:1–5).

The Word of God will bring forth the will of God in the
life of the willing child of God.

David Jeremiah

SAFE IN THE WILL OF GOD

You have need of endurance, so that after you have done the will of God, you may receive the promise.

HEBREWS 10:36

When we have trials in our lives, we always have three choices:

We can endure our trials. Of course, some people make us endure their trials with them. We ask them how they're doing, and they're more than happy to tell us. But when we merely endure our troubles, we run the risk of becoming bitter.

We can just escape. Run! Leave! Get out of there! When we do that, we get away from where we are. But if God hasn't told us to leave, we leave the place where God can help us.

We can enlist our troubles. This is the right thing to do. In other words, we can let God use the crises in our lives to make us better, to help us grow in His way. We can step up on our trouble and move to a higher level.

We all have a natural "flight syndrome" that causes us to think, *If I could just run away!* But when we do that, if we're not careful, we make matters worse instead of better. No matter how difficult our circumstances, the safest place for us is always in the will of God.

FINDING FRIENDS

Faithful are the wounds of a friend, but the kisses of an enemy are deceitful.

PROVERBS 27:6

Some friends are willing to wound you in order to help you: "Faithful are the wounds of a friend, but the kisses of an enemy are deceitful" (Proverbs 27:6). Consider the last part of the verse—the characteristics of an "enemy." Essentially, what to be on the watch for is the flattering lips of a deceiver.

A person who constantly compliments you may not be a faithful friend. The wise person will quickly ask, "Why is this person saying all these nice things?" Sometimes that person has a hidden agenda. Perhaps they want something or are so insecure that fawning over people is the only way they know to find a friend.

So how do you find a faithful friend without being taken in by a flatterer or deceiver? Faithful friends edify, but they don't flatter (Romans 15:2). They are humble and demonstrate love (Ephesians 4:2). They don't always tell you what you want to hear. Instead, they are willing to rebuke you if necessary out of love for you (Proverbs 9:8).

Everyone needs to be close to someone who will ask them the hard questions about their lives. A faithful friend will ask those questions and not rest until he gets the right answers.

David Jeremiah

DEFINING THE GOSPEL

I delivered to you first of all that which I also received: that Christ died for our sins according to the Scriptures, and that He was buried, and that He rose again the third day.

1 CORINTHIANS 15:3–4

Duncan McNeil, the Scottish evangelist, once said that in school he had a seminary professor who insisted on opening his theology classes with a question. No one could ever anticipate what the question would be. One day he said to his students, "Gentlemen, can someone give me a definition of the gospel?"

A student rose and read John 3:16: "For God loved the world so much that he gave his only Son so that anyone who believes in Him shall not perish but have eternal life."

The professor said, "That is a good gospel text, but it is not a definition of the gospel." Another student read 1 Timothy 1:15: "How true it is, and how I long that everyone should know it, that Christ Jesus came into the world to save sinners—and I was the greatest of them all." Again the professor declined to accept it; he waited for what he wanted. Finally, a student stood and read 1 Corinthians 15:3–5, much to the professor's delight. It was evident that he had the reply he desired; he said, "Gentlemen, that is the gospel. Believe it, live it, preach it, and die for it if necessary."

DEO VOLENTE

You ought to say, "If the Lord wills, we shall live and do this or that."
JAMES 4:15

If you have read letters exchanged between Christians a hundred years ago, you may have noticed the postscript, "D.V." These two letters stand for the words *Deo Volente*, which is Latin for "if the Lord wills."

Submission to the will of God is James's proposed alternative to the presumptuous lifestyle of the businessman: "Instead you ought to say, 'If the Lord wills, we shall live and do this or that'" (James 4:15). This would be an acknowledgment that the planners wanted God's direction and approval and would do nothing without it.

Christians generally agree that three basic issues are involved in knowing the will of God. First, there must be a willingness to do God's will when we find it. Second, we must realize that God's will is always in harmony with His Word. And third, we must come to Him earnestly in prayer seeking guidance. These steps will lead us directly into the will of God.

David Jeremiah

IGNORANT WORSHIP

*"You worship what you do not know; we know what we worship,
for salvation is of the Jews."*

JOHN 4:22

As a pastor, I have come to realize that worship is the ultimate priority for which all of us were created. What does it mean to worship?

When Jesus was talking to the Samaritan woman in John 4 about worship He said, "You worship what you do not know." How can you truly worship something without knowing what it is? How do you worship a God you don't know? Paul calls that ignorant worship.

Last Sunday, churches across the country were filled with people who walked in to worship something they did not know. People engaged in ignorant worship, and nothing really happened in their church or in their lives. They went through the external motions without ever really understanding the internal working, and nothing happened because God does not accept ignorant worship.

Worship is knowing God and worshiping Him, and if we do not know God, we cannot worship Him. Make it a priority to know God.

THE STRENGTH OF TENDERNESS

Husbands, likewise, dwell with them with understanding, giving honor to the wife. . . . Be tenderhearted.

1 PETER 3:7–8

In every survey I have seen asking women what is the main thing they need from their husbands, it's always been the same: tenderness. In our John Wayne and Rambo-inspired culture, men are encouraged to maintain a macho-type persona where tenderness and emotion are not to be displayed. In varying degrees and places, tenderness—not to mention tears—has been viewed as a sign of weakness. But from God's perspective nothing could be further from the truth.

Perhaps the greatest impediment to tenderness for men, especially when it comes to praying and pursuing spiritual interests together, is the presumption of weakness. We don't like to see ourselves as helpless, totally dependent on God. And yet often, the greatest sign of strength that a wife is looking for in her husband is the evidence that he is totally dependent on God and not afraid to confess his own need for Him. His vulnerability in that area is what frees his wife to confess her needs, her fears, and her dependence on God as well.

A marriage that is led by a man who loves his wife authentically, sacrificially, deliberately, and unconditionally will be a prosperous marriage, one that mirrors the relationship between Christ and His church.

David Jeremiah

FUELED BY PRAYER

[Pray] always with all prayer and supplication in the Spirit.
EPHESIANS 6:18

I once borrowed a car and as a favor to the owner filled it with gas. That big Oldsmobile station wagon had an ornament on the hood that said "diesel," a sticker on the rear gate that said "Oldsmobile Diesel," and a note on the fuel gauge reading, "Diesel Fuel Only." So naturally I put diesel fuel in the tank. Big mistake, since the owner had recently converted it to gasoline. When it broke down on the main street of a town in New York, I had to explain why I had put diesel fuel into a vehicle with a gasoline engine.

I don't think I'll ever live that down, so I use it as the perfect illustration of Christians. We are human beings, and we have "Human Being" written all over us, but we've been converted into something else. If you try to run your new spiritual self on the old kind of fuel, it won't work. There are a lot of Christians who haven't figured that out yet. The fuel for the Christian life is prayer. Prayer is the energy that makes it possible for the Christian warrior to wear the armor and wield the sword.

You cannot fight the battle in your own power. No matter how talented you are, if you try to fight the spiritual battle in your own strength, you will be defeated.

Repent Where You Are

Remember therefore from where you have fallen; repent and do the first works.

Revelation 2:5

Perhaps we walked with God early in life, or even got all the way through college with our faith intact. But then, through small concessions in our lives, our walk with the Lord began to erode. Little by little, we slipped away from the things that once had been important to us.

What should we do today? How do we get back? We must remember from whence we have fallen. Repent where we are. Go back and repeat the first works. Confess our sin. Acknowledge who we are. And then remember that God loves us.

The good news of the gospel, my friend, is that before the prodigal ever turned his heart toward home, the father had been praying and waiting for him, thinking of what it would be like to embrace him again in his arms.

God will not force Himself upon us. He will not come and drag us out of our situation. But if we will return, He will love us all the way back home.

David Jeremiah

GETTING A GRIP

*Giving all diligence, add to your faith virtue, to virtue knowledge,
to knowledge self-control.*

2 PETER 1:5—6

Most of us would agree that when it comes to the battle for the right kind of living, the biggest enemy is not out there. The biggest enemy is right here—ourselves. That's why the principle of self-control is so very vital. It is that quality which makes it possible to achieve the goals God has set before us.

In the Greek, the word *temperance* is *kratain*. It means "to grab hold of, to grasp." I believe it's the concept from which we get the idiom "Get hold of yourself," which we use when we're talking to someone who is getting too emotional. The word is used only seven times in the New Testament. In almost every situation, it is used to describe the importance of gaining control and reigning over our passions and desires.

The matter of self-control is a battle fought in the mind. The mind controls the passions. The battle is fought in the world of thought. There is no conflict so severe as the conflict one goes through to subdue oneself.

I'd like to suggest that the best way to deal with the struggle for control over your thoughts and passions is focusing your mind upon Jesus Christ.

WHO PRAYS?

Confess your trespasses to one another, and pray for one another.

JAMES 5:16

The ancient historian Eusebius portrayed James as a Nazarite, an Israelite wholly devoted to God (Numbers 6:1–23), whose times of prayer for his nation were frequent and prolonged.

Most of us find it very hard to identify with a man like James. Who do we know who prays so much that he develops knots on his knees? Perhaps the better question might be, "Who do we know who prays—really prays?" That's not an unfair question, nor is it calculated to instill guilt. It reflects the surveys that have been taken by both Christian and secular researchers. It seems Christians today are too busy to pray!

One of the New Testament's strongest passages on prayer is contained in James's final words to his fellow Jewish believers. In James 5:7–12, the word for *patience* is used seven times. In this passage, the word for *prayer* occurs seven times. When patience is required, prayer is the key.

David Jeremiah

FROM THE INSIDE OUT

The heart of the righteous studies how to answer.

PROVERBS 15:28

For many years following the assassination of President John F. Kennedy, people would ask one another, "Where were you when Kennedy was killed?" Now another date and event has replaced all others in the modern era as the subject of the "Where were you?" discussions: September 11, 2001. More than any other event in our day, the terrorist attacks on New York and Washington, D.C., have redefined life for most people. And many people have come to fear that definition.

The only silver lining in this dark cloud of tragedy is that people are asking questions for which only the Bible has answers: What is our world coming to? Why do people do such things? What can we do to keep terror at bay? The answer that every Christian has discovered and every non-Christian needs to know is this: The world cannot be changed, but people can be. When someone asks you the post-9/11 questions, encourage them with the words of a first-century converted terrorist named Paul: the gospel is the power of God for salvation (Romans 1:16).

The only way the world will be changed is the same way individuals are changed: from the inside out.

OCTOBER

≈

*You are in Christ Jesus, who became for us wisdom from
God—and righteousness and sanctification and redemption.*

—1 CORINTHIANS 1:30

JESUS: MAN ABOUT HIS FATHER'S BUSINESS

And He said to them, "Why did you seek Me? Did you not know that I must be about My Father's business?"

LUKE 2:49

Have you ever come home from church and discovered you left a child behind? As your family gathers around the dinner table, your eyes fixate on the empty chair. "Where's Johnny?" you ask. Blank stares and shrugged shoulders reveal the worst—Johnny got left behind.

When Jesus was just twelve years old, He too was left behind at the temple. His parents returned to find Him and discovered Him sitting among the teachers, asking questions. Greatly distressed, His mother asked Him why He had done this to them. He replied, "Did you not know that I must be about My Father's business?" Even at a young age, Jesus knew He had a unique mission to accomplish. Convinced of this, He did not allow people or circumstances to deter Him.

What unique mission has God called you to? Has He commissioned you to a special assignment at home, work, or the church? Whatever it may be, pursue it with all of your heart. Then at the end of your life, you may say as Jesus did, "I have finished the work which You have given Me to do" (John 17:4).

YOUR WORLD NEEDS KINDNESS

Be kind to one another, tenderhearted, forgiving one another, just as God in Christ forgave you.

EPHESIANS 4:32

The world needs kindness. But let's narrow the scope even further. Your world needs kindness. Your home needs kindness. Where people are living in close proximity, kindness sometimes gets lost.

In the New Testament, the language given to the church is given to the home. The church met in the home. When Ephesians 4:32 says, "Be kind to one another, tenderhearted, forgiving one another, even as God in Christ forgave you," that's also directed at the home.

We need to be tenderhearted, kind, and forgiving. The fruit of the Spirit is tested in that laboratory we call the family. If you can make it work there, it will work anyplace on the face of the earth.

GOD ENCOURAGES; YOU SHOULD TOO

Blessed be the God . . . the Father of mercies.

2 CORINTHIANS 1:3

In the New Testament, each member of the triune God (God the Father, God the Son, God the Holy Spirit) places a priority on encouragement.

Paul wrote to the Corinthians, "Blessed be the God . . . the Father of mercies [encouragement]" (2 Corinthians 1:3). In one of his letters to the Thessalonians, Paul reminded his readers that Jesus Christ is also, at the very core of His ministry, an encourager (2 Thessalonians 2:16–17).

And what can we say about the Holy Spirit? "Encourager" is one of His names! The King James Bible says of the Holy Spirit (in John 14 and 16), "However when He the Comforter is come. . . ." The title "Comforter" translates the word *paraklete*, which means "to encourage." When we encourage people, we live out the ministry of the third Person of the Trinity. He is *the* Encourager.

God the Father encourages. God the Son encourages. God the Holy Spirit encourages. We need to be encouragers because encouragement is one of the primary ministries—in fact, it's a priority of our triune God.

David Jeremiah

CHOOSE NOT TO BE LONELY

They should seek the Lord, in the hope that they might grope for Him and find Him, though He is not far from each one of us.

ACTS 17:27

There is a fundamental emptiness in every human being that can only be filled by the presence of God Himself. It is interesting to note that the only time Jesus Christ cried out in loneliness was from the cross, when the Father forsook Him and allowed Him to die as a sacrifice for the world.

Without the presence of God, the most agonizing loneliness will afflict even the strongest person. No person should search for a solution for his loneliness without solving the basic issue of separation from God.

Accepting Jesus Christ, and being filled by His Spirit, is the first step toward overcoming the negative dimensions of loneliness.

GOD IS IN CONTROL

Oh, the depth of the riches both of the wisdom and knowledge of God! How unsearchable are His judgments and His ways past finding out!

ROMANS 11:33

The greatest minds of history have wrestled with the issue of the sovereignty of God versus the free will of humankind. Someday in eternity we may discover how the track of God's sovereignty and the track of our responsibility finally come together. But the way we should look at this is so simple we sometimes miss it: let God take care of His sovereignty, and let us take care of our responsibility. God's sovereignty explains things that humans cannot possibly fathom.

The sovereignty of God in our lives, from our perspective, is like looking at a weaving from the wrong side. We see all the various threads and knots and strands sticking out. We see it from the back side because we do not have the perspective that God has. But someday in eternity, God will take that patchwork we have looked at and haven't understood, and He will turn it around. We will see the beautiful tapestry that has been woven out of our lives. We can spend all our lives trying to figure out why God does this and why God does that. Sometimes we just have to fall back on the fact that God is sovereign and in control. We can rest secure in that truth.

David Jeremiah

THE GREATEST BARGAIN IN THE WORLD

You are in Christ Jesus, who became for us wisdom from God—and righteousness and sanctification and redemption.

1 CORINTHIANS 1:30

The Bible tells us that when we become Christians, we are immediately equipped with the righteousness of Christ. Paul told the Corinthians, "You are in Christ Jesus, who became for us wisdom from God—and righteousness and sanctification and redemption" (1 Corinthians 1:30). When Jesus Christ came down to this earth as the perfect Son of God, He went to the cross and died for you.

As He hung upon the cross, two major things happened. First, He took our sin upon Himself. The Bible says He became sin for us. All the sins of the world were crucified on that cross with Jesus. Second, He imparted righteousness to us. So when we give our lives over to Him, when we put our trust in Him for eternal life, Christ not only forgives our sin, but gives to us His righteousness. We become righteous in Christ Jesus.

You know, that is the greatest bargain the world has ever known. You give up your sin, and you get His righteousness in return. It is the greatest opportunity anybody has ever had, to get rid of your sin and get the righteousness of Christ imputed to your account in return.

CHRIST THE ROCK

For they drank of that spiritual Rock that followed them,
and that Rock was Christ.

1 CORINTHIANS 10:4

You've probably heard this guideline for health and safety: a human being can go forty days without food, four days without water, and four minutes without oxygen. Generally speaking those are good outside limits to keep in mind—under ideal circumstances. If you've just run a marathon, you'll need oxygen in less than four minutes. And if you're wandering across the desert in 110-degree heat, four days without water will seem like an eternity. That's exactly what it felt like to the children of Israel on their way to the promised land.

When they ran out of water, they accused Moses of bringing them out of Egypt to kill them. God told Moses to take the same rod with which he parted the waters of the Red Sea and strike a large rock where they were camped. From that rock flowed water for all of Israel, and they were saved. Centuries later, the apostle Paul said "that Rock was Christ." Indeed, it was He who offered living, spiritual water to all who would believe and be saved (John 4:14). How long can you go without continuing to drink from the Rock that is Christ?

It takes more than an initial drink to survive life's deserts. Drink deeply from Christ the Rock today.

David Jeremiah

UNCONDITIONAL LOVE

A new commandment I give to you, that you love one another;
as I have loved you, that you also love one another.

JOHN 13:34

Francis of Assisi was terrified of leprosy. And one day, in the narrow path that he was traveling, he saw a leper! Instinctively, his heart shrank back, recoiling from the contamination of that loathsome disease. But then he rallied and, ashamed of himself, ran and cast his arms about the sufferer's neck and kissed him and passed on.

How many of us recoil from those who are different? When we meet someone who looks different, belongs to a different class, believes in a different religion, clashes with our personality, or is on a different intellectual level, we automatically withdraw. Rather than looking at these differences as an opportunity to show love, we allow the differences to separate us.

When you come in contact with those who are different, how do you respond? Do you reach out with arms of love, or do you shrink back? Determine today, with God's help, to love others unconditionally, accepting their differences. If this seems especially difficult, remember that God loves you unconditionally! There are no restrictions on His love.

LIFE-CHANGING WISDOM

Incline your ear to wisdom, and apply your heart to understanding.

PROVERBS 2:2

Some years ago, I was at a men's retreat. The speaker issued a challenge to the group, which he said would change our lives: read one chapter of the book of Proverbs each day for a year. Since there are thirty-one chapters in Proverbs, reading a chapter a day would equal reading the whole book each month (reading two chapters on one day in the months with only thirty days). Reading the entire book of Proverbs twelve times in a year, he said, would change our lives.

Well, I accepted his challenge. In fact, I did it more than once. And I remember the incredible impact it had on my life. Almost without fail, I would read a verse in the morning that would have some bearing on an event that took place during that day. The Proverbs of Solomon are the most practical, hands-on truths one could ever hope to find. And to saturate my mind with those truths day after day for a year turned out to be a powerful tonic for my spiritual life.

Anyone who takes seriously the wisdom of the book of Proverbs will experience these blessings, and many more, as a result.

David Jeremiah

COURAGEOUS IN ANY CRISIS

I will go to the king, which is against the law; and if I perish, I perish!
ESTHER 4:16

When your course is righteous, your courage will be reinforced. Esther had the righteous cause. She was to stand before the king and plead for the life of her people. Was she afraid? Undoubtedly.

Courage is not the absence of fear. Courage is persevering in spite of the fear. Courage doesn't mean being oblivious to danger. People who wait for all the courage they need before they act will never act. But those who take the first little step in the process of courageous activity will be given greater strength by God.

The challenges of life will not get much bigger. But building your faith in God can grow you into a giant able to be courageous in any crisis. We build our faith by doing the things that seem hard to us at the time so that we can gain strength to do the really hard things that come to us in the future.

CHOOSE ONE CHAIR

*Whoever therefore wants to be a friend of the world makes himself
an enemy of God.*

JAMES 4:4

When Luciano Pavarotti was a boy, his father introduced him to the wonders of song. He urged Luciano to work very hard to develop his voice. Taking his father's advice, Luciano because a pupil under Arrigo Pola, a professional tenor. He also enrolled in a teachers college. On graduating, he asked his father, "Shall I be a teacher or a singer?" His father replied, "If you try to sit on two chairs, you will fall between them. For life, you must choose one chair."

Luciano chose one. After seven years of study, he made his first professional appearance. After another seven years, he reached the Metropolitan Opera. He went on to say, "Now I think whether it's laying bricks, writing a book—whatever we choose—we should give ourselves to it. Commitment, that's the key. Choose one chair."

In regard to your spiritual life, you must also make a choice. Will you serve God or the world? You cannot be faithful to both. For if you choose to be a friend of the world, you automatically become an enemy of God. There is no room for split alliances, no room for a divided heart. You must choose one chair.

David Jeremiah

THE RETURN OF GEORGE LUCAS

Dear friends, never avenge yourselves. Leave that to God, for he has said that he will repay those who deserve it.

ROMANS 12:19 TLB

The third movie in the *Star Wars* series was originally titled *Revenge of the Jedi*. Several months prior to the release of the film, many promotional materials were sent to movie theaters and chains across the country. Then someone suggested to director George Lucas that if the Jedi knights were indeed agents of goodness and peace, they would not be motivated by revenge.

Lucas thought about it, then agreed. Even though a title change would mean a substantial cost in redesigning film titles and replacing promotional materials, Lucas retitled the film *Return of the Jedi*.

In our culture, vengeance is not an uncommon concept. When someone does us wrong, our immediate reaction is to want to get back at them. If we are to be Christlike, though, we must give up our vengefulness.

GET BUSY FOR GOD

Therefore, brethren, stand fast and hold the traditions which you were taught, whether by word or our epistle.

2 THESSALONIANS 2:15

Paul says, "Therefore, brethren, stand fast and hold the traditions which you were taught, whether by word or our epistle" (2 Thessalonians 2:15). The daily news can discourage us. But in the midst of it all, there is Jesus and His encouragement. We need to cultivate our relationship with Him until He is not just one of the things in our life; He is *the one thing* in our life—the focus of who we are.

"Comfort your hearts and establish you in every good word and work," Paul goes on to say. This is not the time to wear a white robe, sit on a fence, and passively wait for the Lord's return. This is a time to use the powers and energy you have and get busy for God.

The most simple objective of Christians is not only to go to heaven, but to take as many people with us as we can. Share the gospel, teach children, build up one another, strengthen one another, encourage those who are fallen, and reach out to those who are hurting.

In every good work, "occupy till I come" (Luke 19:13 KJV), said the Lord. This is no time for idleness. This is a time for us to seek the truth and live it out every day.

David Jeremiah

REJOICE IN YOUR CHILDREN

Let her who bore you rejoice.

PROVERBS 23:25

There's great joy in children. Almighty God meant for children to be blessings, not burdens. They are our future. We invest in them everything we are and everything we have, and they carry into future generations who we are.

It isn't true that when a person dies, he really dies, because he lives on—not only in the presence of the Lord if he is a Christian, but in the children who live after him. And if those children are born into the family of God, they will carry that influence with them throughout their lives and through their children's lives after them.

God gives us children as blessings, as benedictions, and as graces to life. In fact, the more children you have, the more potential you have for happiness. I know some don't believe that, but it's true.

We need to remember that children are a gift from God. They are God's blessing upon us. That's the truth of the Word of Almighty God.

LIVE TODAY

God said to Moses, "I AM WHO I AM."

EXODUS 3:14

No one ever sank under the burdens of today; but add yesterday and tomorrow to today, and it can capsize your life. Jesus said, "Sufficient for the day is its own trouble."

Dr. Osler, a famous physician of years past, made a helpful observation. He noted how oceangoing vessels were able to seal off various sections of the boat so that a leak could be contained in only one part of the ship. Though damaged, a ship could still make it to safety.

Just so, he suggested, we need to develop the capacity for sealing off the yesterdays and tomorrows that fuel the fires of worry. We need to learn to live in the compartment of today alone.

God is the great "I AM" (Exodus 3:14), not "I WAS" or "I WILL BE." The Christian who lives with Him today, in the present tense, is the one who will be free from worries about yesterday, today, or tomorrow.

LOVE'S ATTITUDE

Paul, a bondservant of Jesus Christ, called to be an apostle, separated to the gospel of God.

ROMANS 1:1

When we meet people for the first time, frequently in addition to stating our name we will identify our occupation or profession. Our identity is closely linked to what we do.

Paul introduced himself in the book of Romans by stating, "Paul, a bondservant of Jesus Christ, called to be an apostle, separated to the gospel of God."

Paul saw everything in his life through the lens of his slavery to Christ. Outwardly, he wrote as a slave of Caesar, but inwardly he considered himself a bondslave to Jesus Christ. To Paul the term *servant* was a title of dignity and humility. There was no greater position than to be a servant of Jehovah God.

We all would do well to remember that God did not save us to become sensations, but rather to become servants.

OUR GOD OF ORDER

You are complete in Him, who is the head of all principality and power.

COLOSSIANS 2:10

It appears from the information in the Bible that Michael is the protecting and fighting angel and Gabriel is the preaching or announcing angel. Each of them has his own job description and carries out God's will in perfection.

Our God is a God of order and organization. That characteristic of God is reflected in the angelic realm. God has set up an authority structure within the universe, within the church, within the family, within human government; and all these lesser authorities are in submission to the greater authority of Christ Himself. The Bible tells us we are complete in Him, "who is the head of all principality and power" (Colossians 2:10).

God is able to respond to our needs and the challenges of our lives because He is a God of power and order. He is able to do what is necessary, and His angels are set up to respond to His every directive.

David Jeremiah

THE DEDICATION OF ONE

If you remain completely silent at this time . . . you and your father's house
will perish. Yet who knows whether you have come to the kingdom
for such a time as this?

ESTHER 4:14

It is hard to believe that one person can make a difference in the course of human events. But if you subtract Esther from the Old Testament, there is no Jewish nation, there is no Jesus Christ, there is no Bible, and there is no hope for humankind because Esther was the link that preserved the Jewish nation.

She was one who consecrated her life to God and did what God wanted her to do. God used Esther to turn the events of the world around.

He may choose to use you in a significant way as well. The dedication of one can make the difference for many.

SEEKING SOLID ROLE MODELS

Receive him therefore in the Lord with all gladness, and hold such men in esteem.
PHILIPPIANS 2:29

When Raphael was painting his famous Vatican frescoes, a couple of cardinals stopped by to watch and criticize. "The face of the apostle Paul is too red," said one. Raphael replied, "He blushes to see into whose hands the church has fallen."

No one needs to remind us that we live in an age of fallen heroes. But maybe instead of spending so much time analyzing our failures, we ought to seek out some solid role models to emulate and then determine to become the same for the generation that is looking to us.

Paul introduces three such people in the last half of Philippians 2. We learn that Paul himself is an example of selflessness. Paul then presents his spiritual son, Timothy, as an example of service. Finally, we are introduced to Epaphroditus as an example of suffering. Paul was an apostle, Timothy was a pastor, and Epaphroditus was a layman. While it is true that Jesus Christ is the Christian's model, these men are presented as model Christians. Jesus poured Himself out in service to God. These men poured themselves out as servants of Jesus Christ!

David Jeremiah

DON'T GIVE THE DEVIL A FOOTHOLD

Do not . . . give place to the devil.

EPHESIANS 4:26–27

It's easy to allow the devil entry into our lives. The King James Version of the Bible translates Ephesians 4:27 as, "Neither give place to the devil." Better is the New American Standard's, "Do not give the devil an opportunity."

But perhaps the most graphic is the New International Version's, "Do not give the devil a foothold." *The American Heritage Dictionary* says that a *foothold* is "a firm or secure position that provides a base for further advancement." All we need do is give the devil a foothold—a little place where he can bide his time and wait for the opportunity to advance further—to ultimately find ourselves in big spiritual trouble.

Unconfessed bouts of anger, pride, deceit, lust, envy—or any sin—may seem small to you, but they are just what the devil is looking for. If need be, confess them now, and purpose to leave no place for the devil to get a foothold in your life.

RIGHTEOUSNESS THROUGH PROPITIATION

He Himself is the propitiation for our sins, and not for ours only but also for the whole world.

1 JOHN 2:2

T his word *propitiation* is one of the great words of the Bible even though it appears only four times in the entire New Testament. The Greek word for *propitiation* translated the Hebrew word which described the mercy seat, the cover of the ark of the covenant, which sat in the Holy of Holies. God was believed to dwell above the ark, between the outstretched wings of the two cherubim at either end of the mercy seat. The ark contained the stone tablets on which were written the Ten Commandments, the Law which man continually broke. But once a year, the high priest would enter the Holy of Holies and sprinkle the blood of a sacrifice over the mercy seat to cover the broken Law. In this act, he made propitiation for the sins of Israel.

As a result of the covering of the mercy seat with blood, God no longer saw the broken Law, but saw instead the blood of the sacrifice. Propitiation was made. In the same way, John wrote, "If anyone sins, we have an Advocate with the Father, Jesus Christ the righteous. And He Himself is the propitiation for our sins, and not for ours only but also for the whole world" (1 John 2:1–2).

David Jeremiah

ERRORS IN JUDGMENT

We all must appear before the judgment seat of Christ, that each one may receive the things done in the body, according to what he has done, whether good or bad.

2 CORINTHIANS 5:10

The judgment seat of Christ is not about the judgment for your sin. The Bible tells us that judgment already took place at the cross of Jesus Christ. There is nothing anyone can ever do to you about your sin because God did it to His Son in your behalf. Christ was condemned for us. That is what we read in Galatians 1:4: "Who gave Himself for our sins, that He might deliver us from this present evil age."

One of the most commonly asked questions about this is, "How can someone have his sins forgiven and still have his works reviewed at the judgment seat of Christ?" Forgiveness is about justification, while rewards are about the things we do as justified people. These are not works that are done for justification. Because each believer must stand before the judgment seat of Christ, we have no right to judge the work of other believers. We do not even know the rewards we're going to receive, so how in the world would we know what rewards anybody else would receive? We do not know enough about anyone else's motive of heart or faithfulness to know what they would even deserve. And I promise you, when it all comes out, there will be a lot of surprises!

The Decree

*[God] canceled out the certificate of debt consisting of decrees against us
and which was hostile to us; and He has taken it out of the way,
having nailed it to the cross.*

Colossians 2:14 NASB

There are two decrees in the book of Esther: the decree of death and the decree of life. One of the things we learn in studying the Bible is that God has a way to save sinners. You can't go to heaven by your own good works. You can't ever be good enough to go to heaven.

The Bible says, "You must be born again." The reason you must be born again is because a decree has been written that the wages of sin is death. The decree has been written that no one can go to heaven with his sin.

God will not overturn that decree. We violate God the day we are born because of our own sin that we inherited. But the good news is that, just as the decree in Persia was overruled by another decree, God has given us another decree. That decree is that if we believe on the Lord Jesus Christ, we will be saved.

David Jeremiah

FELLOW WORKERS FOR CHRIST

I considered it necessary to send to you Epaphroditus, my brother, fellow worker, and fellow soldier, but your messenger and the one who ministered to my need.

PHILIPPIANS 2:25

Epaphroditus was a fellow worker in the body of Christ, which is another reason why Paul was so fond of him. Paul was without question a worker, and he was attracted to others who gave their all to the advancement of the gospel.

In the spirit of love, I must ask you the same thing I ask myself and those whom I pastor in my church: are you a worker? If you are a Christian, I know you are a brother or sister. But I want to know if you've moved beyond that point and become a worker for Christ. Unfortunately, many in the body of Christ today are looking for the church that offers them the most services. Who do they think provides all those services if not workers just like themselves? If they do find a church offering what they are seeking, then they conclude, "This church is large and has everything all together. They don't need me to do anything." That perspective reflects a definite lack of knowledge about the church of Jesus Christ and its needs.

Every church needs its members to be workers.

WHAT ABOUT DOUBT?

Lord, I believe; help my unbelief!

MARK 9:24

Why do you doubt? Have you been influenced by a book? A professor? Another believer? A non-believer? Identifying your doubts and their source will help you understand what you need answers for and why.

Think of the people in the Old Testament whom God greatly used who had doubts when they heard His plans for them—Sarah, Moses, Gideon, and Jeremiah just to name a few. These people were approached by God Himself and they still doubted!

God knew their doubts just as He knows yours and mine. We don't turn our doubts into prayers to God in order to inform God of our doubts. We tell God what we are thinking and feeling about our faith. That makes it more understandable to us as we try to figure out what is going on in our lives.

Go to God with your doubts. He is waiting to hear from you.

David Jeremiah

THE FOCUS OF EVANGELISM

The Lord added to the church daily those who were being saved.

ACTS 2:47

Pastor Charles Swindoll tells about what was, at one time, the greatest evangelistic outreach center in the metropolitan Boston area—a gas station in Arlington. Bob, the owner, had a vision for his work being part of his faith. He provided such honest and dependable service that cars would often be lined up just to buy gas and be serviced at his station. There were no "Jesus Saves" banners, religious sayings or "fish" symbols in sight. Just Bob—a committed Christian who led dozens of people to faith in Christ because of his Christlike life.

Rebecca Pippert has said, "Christians and non-Christians have something in common: We're both uptight about evangelism." People found Christ at Bob's gas station because Christ, not evangelism, was what they encountered. When evangelism, the church, or even Christianity takes the place of Christ, everybody gets uptight. What is your "gas station"? Wherever you encounter non-Christians, ask God to show you how to make Christ, not evangelism, the focus.

Every Christian is a lens through which the world is trying to catch a glimpse of Jesus.

COMPASSION FOR THE HURTING

Rationale

Rejoice with those who rejoice, and weep with those who weep.

ROMANS 12:15

B abe Ruth, one of the most famous baseball players of
all time, finished his career in a slump. According to a
legendary story, he was ridiculed mercilessly one game as he
made his way back to the dugout. The fans continued to boo
and yell obscenities until a little boy jumped the fence and
ran to Babe's side.

The child threw his arms around Babe's legs, crying as
he fiercely hugged him. Moved by the young boy's display
of affection, Ruth gently lifted the boy up into his arms. As
they walked off the field, the man and boy cried together.

This young boy demonstrated the true nature of compassion—he sympathized with the sorrows of another. His
example reminds us that a compassionate man does not stand
detached from the sufferings of others. Rather, he steps into
the world of the hurting and feels the pain and anguish of
the one suffering. And he expresses his compassion through
a sincere concern, through a listening ear, a shed tear.

The world is full of hurting people, many who are longing for a compassionate friend. Will you be that friend?

David Jeremiah

RARE OBJECTIVITY

Then the king said to me, "What do you request?" So I prayed to the God of heaven.

NEHEMIAH 2:4

Charles Swindoll once called wisdom "the God-given ability to see life with rare objectivity and to handle life with rare stability."

Swindoll wrote, "When we operate in the sphere of the wisdom of God . . . we look at life through lenses of perception, and we respond to it in calm confidence. There's a remarkable absence of fear. . . . We can either lose our jobs or we can be promoted in our work, and neither will derail us . . . because we see it with God-given objectivity, and we handle it in His wisdom."

That's the missing factor in many lives today. We're so busy with our problems that we don't pause to seek God's wisdom in handling them, as commanded in James 1:5. But praying for wisdom doesn't always take that long. In Nehemiah 2, King Artaxerxes noticed that Nehemiah seemed troubled, and he asked the reason. "So I prayed to the God of heaven," Nehemiah later recorded, "and I said to the king. . . ." It was an urgent arrow of prayer, shot silently to heaven in the middle of a momentous conversation—and it got the job done.

If you're facing a challenge today, take time to seek God's wisdom.

GOD IS WITH US

Lo, I am with you always, even to the end of the age.

MATTHEW 28:20

Christ is the only Savior of the world. But the Bible tells stories of leaders who, with God's help, "saved" their people. Moses led his people out of Egypt, where they were miserable and enslaved. But after he brought the Ten Commandments down from the mountain where God had given them to him, he saw his people sinning. He had spent days there with God only to return to find the Israelites had not listened to him or to God. As a savior he was alone, and it was his sole duty to bring his people back to God. With God's help Moses was a savior, and he too felt lonely.

Joseph saved the Hebrew people from famine by giving them food that Egypt had stored. Joseph had spent many years alone because his brothers sold him into slavery, and Joseph was also jailed for an offense of which he was not guilty. Joseph, too, had saved the Israelites by following God's orders. But his path was not an easy one; it was often a lonely one.

Christ bore His burden alone on the cross so that He could obtain victory over death for us. Since Christ bore all the agony, loneliness, and sin of the world, we do not have to fear God's forsaking us. God will always be with us, even unto the end of the age.

David Jeremiah

GETTING TO "YES" THE HARD WAY

Whom the LORD loves, He chastens.

HEBREWS 12:6

Until we are faced with the consequences of what we do wrong, we won't even admit it to ourselves. We are the most marvelous people at rationalizing wrongdoing.

In our culture, absolutes are almost gone. We face a major problem in the church today with people doing what is absolutely wrong and having a good case for why it is not so bad. Until we face the penalty for our wrongdoing, we often won't be honest with ourselves.

I think Jonah probably had a good case for not being the right man for the Assyrian job until the gastric juices started working on him in the belly of the fish. Then he started to say, "Well, maybe I am the right man for the job after all."

Some people think that this type of foxhole decision isn't genuine. But just because we say "yes" to God under pressure doesn't mean we aren't being honest. It means we had to get to "yes" the hard way, but we got there all the same.

SELFLESS LOVE

Now abide faith, hope, love, these three; but the greatest of these is love.

1 CORINTHIANS 13:13

Paul tells us that the secret to all of life is love. A love that cares, that goes out of its own way to find what it can do to minister, makes a difference. Love in a kitchen. Love on the football field. Most of all, love selflessly. I have seen people ministering in churches who get no credit for what they do, and yet, behind the scenes, they serve, minister, and work. They have love—love for children, love for the church, and love for the Lord. There are many Christians who give sacrificially. They do it because love in their hearts makes them want to turn away from their own needs and wants and give of themselves and their substance back to God. That is where joy is to be found.

There is one thing I can tell you about selfless love: if you ever get close to it, you will know it because it feels so good. You won't have to tell anybody about it, and if you do, you might lose it in the process. But if you experience it, you will know the joy of it.

David Jeremiah

NOVEMBER

≈

*Rest in the L*ORD, *and wait patiently for Him.*

—PSALM 37:7

BEAUTIFUL HEAVEN

Then I, John, saw the holy city, New Jerusalem, coming down out of heaven from God, prepared as a bride adorned for her husband.

REVELATION 21:2

I read a story once about a little blind girl whose idea of the beauty of the world was based solely on what her parents had told her. A surgical procedure was developed that would allow her to regain her vision, and she regained her eyesight. After her convalescence, the day came for the bandages to be removed from her eyes. The first person she saw was her mother, and after embracing her she went immediately to the door to look outside. For the first time she saw the beauty of creation. She turned to her mother and exclaimed, "Mama, why didn't you tell me it was so beautiful?"

Of course, her mother had done her best to describe the world in the most colorful ways possible, but the fact is, a picture is worth a thousand words. And I think someday when we get to heaven, we are going to have the same reaction that little girl did—"John, why didn't you tell us it was going to be so beautiful?" I do not know that anyone, in the limited space in which John the apostle wrote, could have described heaven any better. But one glimpse of heaven will outstrip all of his words.

David Jeremiah

God's Enduring Mercy

Oh, give thanks to the LORD, for He is good! For His mercy endures forever.
Psalm 106:1

God's mercy is a recurring theme in the Scriptures. God's grace is God giving us what we do not deserve, and God's mercy is withholding from us what we really do deserve.

Sometimes I hear even Christian people talking about getting their rights. I, for one, don't want my rights. I know what I deserve and it is not something I would like to have. I am grateful for the mercy of God.

Isn't it a matter of His goodness that when man sinned in the garden, God didn't just completely give up on humanity? Isn't it a matter of His goodness that when humankind failed (and when we fail), God didn't immediately withdraw all of the joys and privileges of life? When we wake up in this beautiful world and compare it to what we know we deserve, we should sing with the psalmist, "Oh, give thanks to the Lord, for His mercy and His goodness endure forever!"

STRAIGHT LINES

Moreover, as for me, far be it from me that I should sin against the LORD in ceasing to pray for you.

1 SAMUEL 12:23

D o you know someone who is heading the wrong way? Someone struggling with an overwhelming problem or temptation?

Pray—earnestly pray—for that one. The prophet Samuel told the Israelites, "Moreover, as for me, far be it from me that I should sin against the LORD in ceasing to pray for you" (1 Samuel 12:23). J. Sidlow Baxter pointed out that our loved ones may "spurn our appeals, reject our message, oppose our arguments, despise our persons, but they are helpless against our prayers."

In Colossians 4, we meet a man whose prayers for others were so powerful that he received special commendation in the Bible: Epaphras . . ."a bondservant of Christ, greets you, always laboring fervently for you in prayers, that you may stand perfect and complete in all the will of God" (v. 12).

Oswald Chambers said, "By intercessory prayer we can hold off Satan from other lives and give the Holy Ghost a chance with them. No wonder Jesus put such tremendous emphasis on prayer!"

David Jeremiah

LOVE IN THE LITTLE THINGS

There should be no schism in the body, but . . . the members should have the same care for one another.

1 CORINTHIANS 12:25

Courtesy is one of those things that is so simple we forget about it. Most of us want to get involved in the large, huge, loving things. But you see, courtesy isn't the great big love involvement. Courtesy is love in the little things. Courtesy is the simplicity of love.

You can take the most untutored person and put him into the highest society, and if he has a reservoir of courteous love, he will not behave unwisely. A person who is committed to God's kind of love, as simple as he may be, will know what to do and will be accepted. Carlisle said of Robert Burns that there was no truer gentleman than the plowman poet. "He loved everything, and all things great and small that God had made. So with this simple passport he could mingle with any society and enter courts and palaces from his little cottage, and be accepted."

I've known people like that. Maybe they don't have the right clothes or don't know just the right words to say, but because of their simplicity and their easiness with people and their courtesy in conversation, they seem to be accepted in any strata of society. That is the simplicity of love.

A Need-to-Know Basis

As the heavens are higher than the earth, so are My ways higher than your ways, and My thoughts than your thoughts.

Isaiah 55:9

The more I study, the more I discover I don't know—and I study all the time! I continually pray that God would give me greater capacity to learn and know about Him. But I accept the fact that I will never know it all—and so should you. There are definite limitations to what we have the capacity and intelligence to understand.

The Bible has everything you need to know in order to know God and receive eternal life, through faith in His Son. If you have other questions that are answered in the Bible, all the better. But if the Bible doesn't have the answers, don't doubt the answers the Bible does have.

There is so much about the universe and the God who made it that we simply do not know. The bottom line is that we will never understand God and all of His ways.

God's purposes, and what He has revealed to us of them, are moving ahead on His timetable. And He has told us what we need to know, to make sure we are safely on board. Let's learn to trust God with the things we do not understand.

David Jeremiah

PUTTING OTHERS FIRST

Let each of you look out not only for his own interests,
but also for the interests of others.

PHILIPPIANS 2:4

Theodore Roosevelt's child once jabbed, "Father always had to be the center of attention. When he went to a wedding, he wanted to be the bride. When he went to a funeral, he was sorry that he couldn't be the corpse."

Although we may find humor in this illustration, it reflects a harmful "me-first" philosophy. This philosophy can best be defined by the motto "Look out for number one." Self is enthroned as king; people, circumstances, and life are subjects that must bow down. After all, every individual deserves to be happy. Embracing this philosophy, self becomes the epicenter of the world. But according to God's Word, self is not to be the focal point of our lives. God's plan is for us to focus our thoughts, time, and energy on loving Him and others (Matthew 22:36–39).

If you were to write your life motto, what would it say? Look out for number one? Or look out for the needs of others? Ask God to help you live a selfless life.

PERSONAL ACCOUNTABILITY TO HIM

On the first day of the week let each one of you lay something aside, storing up as he may prosper.

I CORINTHIANS 16:2

There is a rumor afoot that God holds churches accountable for how much they give. But that's all it is—a rumor. That's not the truth. In no place does the Bible even hint that God holds a church accountable for its giving. However, God does operate on an individual accountability basis. And that's very clear in Scripture.

When we give ourselves to God first, we understand that we are accountable to Him as His people. The Bible says we are to lay aside each week that which God has entrusted to us. And we are reminded over and over in the New Testament that someday we are to give an account to God for what we have done.

If I have given myself to God first, if I have said, "God, everything that I am, everything that I have belongs to You," then I don't really have to live in fear of that day of accountability. I've already had my day of accountability. I've stood before God the best I know how and said, "God, You direct me, and I'll be a channel for whatever You put in my hands. I am going to be accountable to You as You tell me in Your Word You want me to be."

David Jeremiah

TRUST GOD FOR EVERYTHING

Your heavenly Father knows that you need these things.

MATTHEW 6:32

When we read about the widow in Mark 12, we see a woman who trusted completely in God, who gave everything she had to Him because she knew He would care for her. Perhaps if we were to examine our own hearts, we would find that the reason we are reluctant to give is not so much a matter of treasure as it is a matter of trust. We have entrusted God with our eternal souls, but we are unwilling to trust Him with our temporal riches.

I heard about a man who complained to his pastor about not having any money left over for God after paying his bills. The pastor asked him, "Would you be willing to trust God to take care of you, tithe every month, and bring me whatever bills you can't pay?" Of course, the man quickly agreed to that plan, but that led the pastor to say, "It's strange you would trust me, an imperfect man, to care for your needs, but you will not trust Almighty God, who demonstrated His love for you by sending His Son to die on a cross." When it comes right down to it, we either trust God to take care of us, or we trust in our money.

AUDIT YOUR ANGER

Let all bitterness, wrath, anger, clamor, and evil speaking be put away from you.

EPHESIANS 4:31

Anger turns into resentment, resentment turns into bitterness, bitterness turns into unforgiveness, and unforgiveness turns into a defiled conscience. Pretty soon, we have become captives of our own anger.

Anger is nothing more than a sophisticated version of a temper tantrum. Just because we can define it with eloquent speech doesn't mean it is any more justified. We are still mad that we can't get what we want. And our anger overflows out of us and defiles everyone around us.

Instead of nursing, rehearsing, conversing about, and dispersing our anger, we need to reverse our anger before it hurts us and others.

How do you reverse anger? Paul says you do it with forgiveness and loving-kindness and tenderness. You go to the person toward whom you have directed your anger, and you seek forgiveness.

David Jeremiah

EVERYTHING COMES FROM GOD

For all things come from You, and of Your own we have given You.

1 CHRONICLES 29:14

James 1:17 tells us that every good and perfect gift comes from the Father. It isn't earned; it's something He decides to give. That's why Deuteronomy 8:18 warns us to remember the Lord, "for it is He who gives you power to get wealth." A businessman may think he is a self-made man, but the very power to succeed came from God. As Paul said in 1 Timothy 6:7 and 17, "For we brought nothing into this world, and it is certain we can carry nothing out. . . . [It is] God who gives us richly all things to enjoy."

After one of the greatest offerings in history, King David had to actually tell the people to stop giving because they had given so much. After he had received the offering, David prayed these words, recorded in 1 Chronicles 29:14: "For all things come from You, and of Your own we have given You." I love those words, for they remind me that anything I give to God is merely a giving back of His own abundant blessing. I'm simply giving back to God what He already owns.

SPEAK TO YOUR "ABBA FATHER"

Abba, Father, all things are possible for You.

MARK 14:36

C alling God "Abba" is rooted in Jesus' agony in the Garden of Gethsemane: "And He said, 'Abba, Father, all things are possible for You. Take this cup away from Me; nevertheless, not what I will, but what You will'"(Mark 14:36).

Abba was an ordinary family word of Jesus' day. It conveyed intimacy, tenderness, dependence, and complete lack of fear or anxiety. Modern English equivalents would be Daddy or Papa.

No Jew would have dreamed of using this very intimate term to address God. However, Jesus always used this word in His prayers (Aramaic *abba* or its Greek equivalent *pater*), with the exception of His cry from the cross.

And Jesus instructed His disciples to use this word in their prayers as well. We are empowered to speak to God just as a small child speaks to His father.

David Jeremiah

WE CAN'T FOOL OUR KIDS

A disciple is not above his teacher, but everyone who is perfectly trained will be like his teacher.

LUKE 6:40

We can't fool our kids. At home, you and I are the real you and I. "Do as I say, not as I do" won't cut it. What we do is so powerful that it can destroy everything we say. We had better live out what we say we believe from the Word of God, or our words will act more like poison than fertilizer in the soil of our children's hearts.

If we don't model a real, genuine relationship with Jesus Christ, there's little chance our children will grow up to possess what we lack.

For many reasons, King David is revered by millions today, centuries after he ruled Israel. He gave his children all they needed, except an example they could follow. As we trace the pattern in David's family, we see David's children repeating the same mistakes their father made. His serious errors stripped him of the power to restrain his children.

Does this mean we have to be perfect? Of course not. But our children can see the genuineness of who we are in Christ as we trust the Lord each day.

THE GREAT PHYSICIAN

May your whole spirit, soul, and body be preserved blameless at the coming of our Lord Jesus Christ.

1 THESSALONIANS 5:23

Is there no balm in Gilead?" asked Jeremiah. "Is there no physician there? Why then is there no recovery for the health of . . . my people?" (Jeremiah 8:22).

Gilead, a region east of the Jordan, was famous for its medicinal salve, but Jeremiah warned that not even Gilead's balm could heal the soul.

But the Great Physician can heal. He can give physical healing, and we should pray for one another to be healed (James 5:16). God sometimes heals miraculously and other times through medical science. Sometimes He doesn't grant physical healing because He has other plans and purposes for us (2 Corinthians 12:8–9).

He can give emotional healing. When Jeremiah was devastated by the terror of war, he felt like a man mangled by a lion or trapped in a tomb. But as he recalled God's unfailing mercy, hope returned to his heart (Lamentations 3:6, 10, 21–24).

The Lord can give spiritual healing. "The chastisement for our peace was upon Him, and by His stripes we are healed" (Isaiah 53:5).

Whatever your need, the Great Physician now is near, the sympathizing Jesus.

David Jeremiah

REST IN THE LORD

Rest in the LORD, and wait patiently for Him.

PSALM 37:7

What does it mean to rest in the Lord? Let me use a familiar illustration. When you enter your church on Sunday morning and go to a particular pew or chair to take your seat, you probably do not give one second's thought to whether that pew or chair is going to hold your weight when you sit on it. Why is that? Simply because you have grown accustomed to the fact that you do not have to worry about the seats holding your weight. Week after week, the seats in your church have been found faithful. At some point, those seats passed the test in your mind, and you have never given them another thought.

You can develop the same kind of confidence in God. By trusting and delighting in Him, you can learn to rest in Him as well. With each problem that arises, you can exercise confidence that He will be faithful to meet your needs. You, by resting, will be unmovable in your place of faith because day after day, week after week, year after year, you have entered into His presence and given over to Him the cares of your life.

RENEW YOUR MIND

Do not be conformed to this world, but be transformed by the renewing of your mind.

ROMANS 12:2

The only way to survive in a world that tries to slowly poison our minds is to renew our minds each day. The psalmist says in Psalm 1 that the blessed man is the one who delights in the law of the Lord, meditating on it day and night. When I open my Bible for personal devotions, I know that I'm looking at the very Word of God. It's different from everything else around me. What I'm reading is in a whole different universe. I'm getting a transfusion of heavenly culture into my system. I know that if I try to make it in this world, I'll get pulled down. I'll never be happy following the world's plan.

But when I came to Jesus Christ, the happiness of this world was ruined for me. I've got the Holy Spirit inside me, and I can never be happy unless I'm walking with Him. People can try to be happy, but they'll never achieve it apart from the Lord. Christians can try to follow the world's plan for happiness, but the only way they will find it is to let the Word of God cleanse and renew them.

David Jeremiah

FAITHFULNESS IN MINISTRY

You heard and knew the grace of God in truth; as you also learned from Epaphras, our dear fellow servant who is a faithful minister of Christ on your behalf.

COLOSSIANS 1:6–7

In Colossians 1:7, Paul not only calls Epaphras a dear fellow servant, but a "faithful minister of Christ." Here is another key characteristic of those God uses: faithfulness. When was the last time you heard someone in the body of Christ commended for being so faithful? We speak well of almost every other trait before we think of faithfulness. Yet, in truth, faithfulness in ministry underlies everything else we do for Christ. It's easy to be faithful in moments of crisis or great need, but I'm talking about those who labor faithfully for the Lord, day in and day out, with little notice. Faithfulness translates into persistence in ministry.

The persistent minister is the one who makes it to the finish line. Teaching Sunday school? Leading a backyard Bible club? Singing in the choir? Serving as a deacon? Faithfulness in these or any other ministry means you will take your last step as you cross the finish line—and not before. Epaphras was that kind of man—a faithful minister of Christ.

THE PEARLY GATE

We love Him because He first loved us.

1 JOHN 4:19

Why does God love us? Not because we're lovable by nature. Deuteronomy 7:7–8 offers this remarkable answer: "The LORD did not set His love on you nor choose you because you were more in number than any other people, for you were the least of all peoples; but because the LORD loves you. . . ." Read that again! "The LORD . . . set His love on you . . . because . . . the LORD loves you." He loves us just because He loves us. His nature is to love.

Why do we love God? Not because we are loving by nature. First John 4:19 offers a remarkable answer: "We love Him because He first loved us." Our love is responsive. William Tyndale, who was later burned at the stake for translating the Bible into English, was a brilliant, winsome scholar whose life was changed by finding 1 John 4:19 in the Greek New Testament. He called it "the pearly gate through which I entered the Kingdom." Tyndale wrote, "I used to think that salvation was not for me, since I did not love God; but those precious words showed me that God does not love us because we first loved Him. No, no; we love Him because He first loved us. It makes all the difference!"

David Jeremiah

THE DANGER OF UNBELIEF

He did not do many mighty works there because of their unbelief.

MATTHEW 13:58

Unbelief is the greatest obstacle to the expression of faith in the life of Christians. Unbelief has ruined the vision of more people than any other single characteristic. One of the reasons so many churches settle for mediocrity is because they are limited by their unbelief.

We ought to pray every day, both corporately and as individuals, that God would never limit us through our own unbelief. Sometimes we set barriers on our lives because we won't believe great things. Matthew 13:58 tells of Jesus coming to Nazareth and not doing many miracles "because of their unbelief." The greatest problem we face in churches is the problem of unbelief. Doubt creeps into the hearts of those who should be walking in faith and trusting God for His provision.

Unbelief settles into their lives like a dark cloud, wiping out God's plan and destroying the opportunity for His miracle-making power to take place. There will always be confrontation with unbelief for anyone willing to do great things for God.

PRIDE—THE ORIGINAL SIN

God resists the proud, but gives grace to the humble.

JAMES 4:6

I f there is a deadly sin, one that is more wicked than any other, it has to be pride. James 4:6 tells us, "God resists the proud, but gives grace to the humble." God resists the proud. The one thing that seems to turn the power of God off in a person's life more than anything else is pride.

Pride is the original sin, if there is such a thing. It goes all the way back to when Satan was separated from God. Isaiah 14:12–14 says, "How you are fallen from heaven, O Lucifer, son of the morning! . . . For you have said in your heart: 'I will ascend into heaven. I will exalt my throne above the stars of God; . . . I will ascend above the heights of the clouds, I will be like the Most High.'"

And God said, "I have had enough of Lucifer!" Next thing we know, the separation has occurred and Satan and his demons are gone. With all of the difficulties and problems that God brings into our lives, things we would never choose for ourselves, I wonder sometimes if they are simply God's messengers to keep our feet on the ground and away from a proud heart.

David Jeremiah

Paying the Piper

Be sure your sin will find you out.

Numbers 32:23

The great news of the gospel is that we have a forgiving God. When we come to Him, open our hearts, and confess our sins, God does hear us and forgive us. He's just waiting for us to come and ask Him. God puts confessed sins behind His back as far as the east is from the west. He buries them in the deepest sea.

God forgets what He forgives. Yet there's a postscript: the Lord won't erase history. Some consequences may be set in motion while we are out of fellowship with God, and we must reap what we sow. Even when we have been restored to fellowship through the forgiveness process, sometimes we have to "pay the piper."

It is impossible to get away with sin. You can't do it. Numbers 32:23 says it this way: "Be sure your sin will find you out." Just as surely as you can't get away with sin, you can't get away from God's love. No matter how evil your conduct, God loves you. The reason you have that hurt in your heart right now is because you're God's, and He doesn't want you out of fellowship with Him.

TRAIL OF BLOOD

The things you have heard . . . commit these to faithful men who will be able to teach others also.

2 TIMOTHY 2:2

Long before Martin Luther "discovered" Reformation truth, John Hus was preaching it in Behemia (Czech Republic). Born about 1373 of peasant parentage, Hus became the most powerful preacher in Prague. He advocated reform in the church, which drew the displeasure of his fellow clergy. When he declared Scripture alone sufficient for Christian life and practice, he was summoned before the Council of Constance.

On July 6, 1415, Hus was found guilty of heresy, condemned, and taken to the outskirts of town to be burned. His last words were, "I have never thought nor preached except with the intention of winning men, if possible, from their sins. In the truth of the gospel I have written, taught, and preached; today I will gladly die."

It's dangerously easy to sit in church and yawn over the very truths for which earlier generations died. Our Bibles have been passed to us at great cost. Take a few moments today to thank God for the faithfulness of those who have handed down to us the gospel, and rededicate yourself to passing it along to someone else.

JUDGE YOUR OWN SIN

For if we would judge ourselves, we would not be judged.

1 CORINTHIANS 11:31

When I was a boy, I worked at a place where I could get the autograph of some pretty famous Christians, and they would always put a favorite Scripture reference under their name. One time a man signed his name and wrote underneath it, "1 Corinthians 11:31." I didn't know that verse, so that night I found it and read the words, "For if we would judge ourselves, we would not be judged." If we take note of the sin in our lives and take the initiative to put it behind us, then the Bible says we won't be judged for that sin. But then the converse thought occurred to me: if there is unconfessed sin our lives, and we refuse to deal with it, God will have to judge that sin.

None of us can make it through this life without sinning. The road of life is rough, and there are ruts and potholes in which we can fall. But the Bible tells us how to deal with the sin in life: repent and confess it. If we do, God will bless. If we don't, God will judge. The choice is ours.

TRAIN UP A CHILD

Train up a child in the way he should go, and when he is old he will not depart from it.

PROVERBS 22:6

Each child needs to know that he is unique and not like any other child God ever created. The Hebrew phrase "in the way" describes the habit or character of an individual at his own age level. The emphasis is on the importance of adjusting our training according to the ability of the child at each stage of his development. Each child has his own way, and by paying attention, we can determine what that way is.

The root meaning for the term *train up* is 'palate or roof of the mouth.' The Arab midwife would take olive oil or crushed dates on her finger and rub the palate of a newborn baby to create in the infant a desire to suck. A real meaning of "training" is to create a taste or desire. Our task is to develop in our children a hunger or desire for spiritual things, to cultivate an urge to follow God.

THE MASTER KEY TO SPIRITUAL GROWTH

For whoever has, to him more will be given, and he will have abundance: but whoever does not have, even what he has will be taken away from him.

MATTHEW 13:12

Jesus explained in Matthew 13:12:"For whoever has, to him more will be given, and he will have abundance; but whoever does not have, even what he has will be taken away from him."

This is the great principle upon which God operates in human lives today, the master key to our spiritual growth. This principle is so fundamental that it applies to other things besides spiritual truth. For instance, while I was in college, I broke both my ankles within a period of about a year and a half. After having a cast on my ankle and calf, and removing it, I discovered my calf had shrunk dramatically in size compared to the one without a cast. Why? Because the muscles in the calf had atrophied from lack of use. Everything that is not used is ultimately lost.

Jesus was giving His disciples a principle: those who have responded to what they have been given will get more and continue to grow. But those who have not responded to what they have been given will find what they have decreasing until it is removed altogether. Lack of revelation from God is due to lack of willingness to receive it.

ETERNAL PROFIT FROM OUR PAIN

For they indeed for a few days chastened us as seemed best to them,
but He for our profit, that we may be partakers of His holiness.

HEBREWS 12:10

When Jacob was an old man, the Lord commanded him to move to Bethel, and Jacob finally decided to obey God. He met the Lord face-to-face, after having fought Him his whole life, and the result was that, in his old age, Jacob finally stopped resisting.

God will not spare present pain if it means eternal profit. God is more concerned with our spiritual growth than our temporal comfort, so He allows adversity to help us grow. God perseveres with us, even when we have given up on ourselves. What the Lord starts, He finishes. Jacob was an unlovely person, but God loved Him anyway. God's priority for our lives does not include a Jacob-like experience. God's will for our lives is to obey Him, not run away so that He has to discipline us.

Jacob's son Joseph learned those lessons. When he was called by God to obey, he obeyed willingly. The difference between his life and that of his father is stunning—and particularly insightful. It pays to serve the Lord.

David Jeremiah

PEACE IN TURMOIL

Let not your heart be troubled, neither let it be afraid.

JOHN 14:27

Jesus said, "Let not your heart be troubled." He spoke these words to His disciples on a night when He knew that, in a matter of hours, the lives of His disciples would be permanently impacted through His own terrible ordeal and death.

He told them the Holy Spirit would come as a Comforter. He told them a place was being prepared for them. He told them He would come again and receive them unto Himself. He told His disciples that they could have peace in the midst of turmoil if they would receive the peace He gives.

All too often we lose our peace in the midst of tragedy and the circumstances of life. When we do that, we have nothing to offer a watching world. If a neighbor comes to us distraught over tragedy and finds us just as undone, what testimony have we given about the peace of Christ that He promised? It is the Christians in a community who should be able to offer a word of encouragement and comfort during difficult times. But we can only do that if we possess the peace of Christ—that peace He purchased for us at the price of His own blood.

With Open Hands

*Give, and it will be given to you: good measure, pressed down, shaken together,
and running over will be put into your bosom.*

Luke 6:38

When Elijah met the widow of Zarephath, she was locked in the clutches of a handful of meal and a tiny bit of oil. That's all she had. We can sympathize with her. In fact, some of us can identify with her. And Elijah's heart went out to her.

The difference was that he knew something she didn't know. He knew that the way to have what you have and have it to the fullest is to always put God first. That's why he said, "Make me a little cake first." In other words, "Trust God by putting Him first and watch what He does."

When we first see this woman in the story, she is clutching everything she has. At the end of the story, she is releasing it all to God. The way to have what you have is to give it back to God. That is the only way you can ever possess your possessions. If you give it back to God with open hands, He will not only bless you, He will also put back what you need.

David Jeremiah

COMPARED WITH WHAT?

We do not care to classify or compare ourselves with some who commend themselves. When they measure themselves by themselves and compare themselves with themselves, they are not wise.

2 CORINTHIANS 10:12 NIV

I'm always a little surprised when I hear someone comment that they cannot understand why God would do something for Mr. and Mrs. Someone and not for them. But the comment that shocks me is when they say, "It isn't fair."

The hard truth is, we ought to be asking why God would ever do anything for any of us. As Jeremiah wrote, "Through the LORD's mercies we are not consumed, because His compassions fail not" (Lamentations 3:22). The only thing we "deserve" is His wrath. Whatever talent or ability we may develop or position we may achieve, it is only because of God's great grace.

I love Paul's gentle sarcasm when he writes: "We do not dare to classify or compare ourselves with some who commend themselves. When they measure themselves by themselves and compare themselves with themselves, they are not wise" (2 Corinthians 10:12 NIV). Today, thank Him for who you are and every blessing He has provided.

PRAYER MAKES US BETTER

[Give] thanks always for all things to God the Father in the name of our Lord Jesus Christ.

EPHESIANS 5:20

I t is not new truth to many of us that prayer is a great comfort in uneasy times and a mighty warrior against worry. I am convinced, however, that we are confused about the way prayer actually works for us in such stressful and difficult days.

Does Paul's call to prayer mean that when we pray, all the things we worry about will be straightened out for us and that our trouble will be gone? Not necessarily!

If prayer does not always change our situation so that it no longer worries us, then what is the value of praying? Here is the answer! Prayer does not always change the situation and make it better, but prayer always changes us and makes us better.

Prayer, especially prayer accompanied by thanksgiving, is the perfect answer to a heart that is overridden with anxiety.

David Jeremiah

PROBLEM OR PULPIT?

*The things which happened to me have actually turned out
for the furtherance of the gospel.*

PHILIPPIANS 1:12

Samuel Rutherford attended Edinburgh University as a young man and began teaching there at age twenty-three. But desiring to preach the gospel, he assumed the pastorate in Anwoth, Scotland, in 1627, and served faithfully for ten years. In 1636, he was called before the High Commission Court to defend his Puritan views. He lost the case and was exiled from his congregation.

On July 13, 1637, he wrote to his church from exile: "Next to Christ, I had but one joy, the apple of the eye of my delights, to preach Christ my Lord; and they have violently plucked that away from me. It was to me like the poor man's one eye; and they have put out that eye, and quenched my light in the inheritance of the Lord." But all this actually furthered the gospel. While in exile, he wrote many letters which were later compiled into one of Christian history's greatest classics, *The Letters of Samuel Rutherford*.

Whenever you experience a reversal in life, look around for an opportunity to share the gospel. Problems have a way of becoming pulpits in the overruling providence of God.

DECEMBER

God is our refuge and strength.

—PSALM 46:1

ONE PLUS GOD

I sought for a man among them who would make a wall, and stand in the gap before Me on behalf of the land, that I should not destroy it; but I found no one.

EZEKIEL 22:30

When Frances Havergal, author of the hymn "Take My Life and Let It Be," was a teenager, her parents moved to Dusseldorf, Germany, where she was placed in a German school. She was the only Christian among 110 pupils. The others made fun of her, teased her, even persecuted her. Her response? "It was very bracing," she wrote. "I felt I must try to walk worthy of my calling, for Christ's sake. It was a sort of nailing my colors to the mast."

You might be the only Christian in your school, on your ball team, at your office, or in your family. What an opportunity! Christians are the "salt of the earth." It doesn't take a lot of salt to season the whole pot. The presence of even one believer can hinder sin, delay judgment, prompt conviction, and extend the kingdom of God.

Paul and his two companions were apparently the only believers on the storm-tossed ship in Acts 27. But their presence saved all 276 people on board. The odds against Elijah on Mount Carmel were 450 to one, but *one plus God is a majority*. The feeblest light is best seen in the thickest darkness. Don't be afraid to nail your colors to the mast.

David Jeremiah

THE MISSING JEWEL

He is your Lord, worship Him.

PSALM 45:11

Once A. W. Tozer called worship the "missing jewel" of the modern church. There are too many churches, too many Christians that do not know how to worship God, or even why worship is our primary responsibility before Him. We have churches that emphasize preaching, churches that stress evangelism, and churches that highlight body fellowship, but worship is the priority commandment from God. We are called to love the Lord our God with all our heart, soul, mind, and strength, and we develop our love for Him in worship.

Our lives are changed and our spiritual walk is strengthened as we come before God and worship Him. It is the priority commandment in His Word. We will never truly know God until we worship Him, and we will never really worship Him unless we know Him. He is sitting on the throne in heaven, worthy of honor and glory and praise, awaiting our worship. He inhabits the praises of His people and can be found there with them as they worship Him. He is a great God, a King above all gods who will be gloriously worshiped throughout all eternity. And He wants you to know Him.

IN TRAGEDIES AND TRIUMPHS

But as for you, you meant evil against me; but God meant it for good, in order to bring it about as it is this day, to save many people alive.

GENESIS 50:20

One of the greatest assets Joseph had was his sensitivity to every situation. In both his triumphs and tragedies, Joseph was able to see through his circumstances and see God at work behind the scenes.

Joseph always seems to be conscious of God in his life. He refused the invitation of Potiphar's wife because he recognized that it would be "a sin against God." He refused to exalt himself when interpreting Pharaoh's dream, instead insisting that "God shall give Pharaoh an answer." Now he refuses to take vengeance upon his brothers for selling him as a slave, since he now knows the Lord had it in mind all along. Joseph made God part of every aspect of his life.

If we can come to a place in our spiritual walk where we can see God at work in both our triumphs and tragedies, we'll find new peace in our souls. We don't always understand or particularly like what God arranges, but we understand the fact that He is in charge, and we bow to His sovereignty. That's called living with an eternal perspective, and it's exactly what Joseph does. He has confidence that God is at work on His master plan, regardless of how the immediate circumstances appear.

David Jeremiah

COME TO ME

Come to Me, all you who labor and are heavy laden, and I will give you rest.
MATTHEW 11:28

Stress is the catchall disease of our day. It is blamed for medical conditions and just about anything else that people don't know how to otherwise explain. Huge sums of money are spent every year to teach people how to live with stress.

Two thousand years ago, a book was written under the inspiration of God the Holy Spirit that purports to have the answers to all of mankind's needs. Can a book written so long ago really speak to the modern age in which we live? See if Jesus' words in Matthew 11:28–30 aren't the perfect invitation to the stressed-out people of our day: "Come to Me, all you who labor and are heavy laden, and I will give you rest. Take My yoke upon you and learn from Me, for I am gentle and lowly in heart, and you will find rest for your souls. For My yoke is easy and My burden is light."

The invitation, though two thousand years old, is still valid because the basic human need is still the same: people are still weary from the process of living life without God.

NEED A LIFT?

Now my head shall be lifted up above my enemies all around me.

PSALM 27:6

Have you ever seen people with so much trouble that their heads are down? Have you felt that way? You face a confrontation and it goes wrong. You walk away from there with your head down. Very graphic, isn't it? The Bible says that when you face trouble and you worship, that worship becomes the lifter of your head. You could walk into church with the burdens of the world on you, and when you get caught up in the worship of the Lord, it's almost like God just lifts your head right up.

Worship makes God big in your heart. Is God big? Yes. He can't get any bigger than He is. I mean, God is God. But worship magnifies God; it puts awareness of who God is into your heart so you begin to sense and appreciate the greatness of Almighty God. When you see His greatness and you put your trouble in that picture, everything changes. When you measure your trouble against others, you might be depressed, but when you measure your trouble against the greatness and magnificence of God, that's encouraging. No wonder your head gets lifted!

David Jeremiah

SEEKING, NOT JUST TENDING

The Son of Man has come to seek and to save that which was lost.

LUKE 19:10

We are all familiar with the idea of equipping the saints to do the work of the ministry (Ephesians 4:12)—and that is certainly part of our responsibility. But I think if the Lord Jesus were in the average Bible-believing church, He would want to know why we spend so much time trying to meet our own needs when there are so many lost sheep out there who don't know God.

I love the ministry of the church I pastor, and yet I sometimes wonder if our church is not doing as much seeking and saving of the lost as we should be. Sometimes we are like Old Testament armies who come upon the spoils of a battle and gorge themselves instead of sharing with others.

I think Jesus is telling us in this parable that, while it is nice to be part of the ninety-nine sheep who are already safe inside the sheepfold, we ought to keep looking for the lost ones. Remembering what it means personally to be found is a great motivation for going to find others.

LOVE NEVER FAILS

Love never fails.

1 CORINTHIANS 13:8

Eusebius, the "father of church history," wrote how the early Christians demonstrated love during plagues and epidemics: "Most of our brethren showed love and loyalty in not sparing themselves while helping one another, tending to the sick with no thought of danger, and gladly departing this life after becoming infected with their disease. Many who nursed others to health died themselves."

He then added, "The heathen were the exact opposite. They pushed away those with the first signs of the disease and fled from their dearest."

Philippians 2:4 gives a great definition of love: "Let each of you look out not only for his own interests, but also for the interests of others." Love is seeking the best of the one loved. It is meeting the needs of another without thought of our own. It is doing for another what we would like to have done for ourselves (Matthew 7:12).

On a very practical level, this involves a lot of little things—sharing housework with your spouse, remaining patient with your children, listening to a friend, sharing praise with a co-worker, helping a neighbor in need, or maybe just holding your tongue when you'd rather let loose. This kind of love never fails.

David Jeremiah

LISTEN TO OTHERS

Let every man be swift to hear, slow to speak, and slow to wrath, for the wrath of man does not produce the righteousness of God.

JAMES 1:19–20

It is unfortunate that when we think about communication, we only think of the active aspect of communication, which is talking. We ought also to consider the important passive application of communication, which is listening. Experts tell us that it is not easy to teach people to listen, but it is a skill that can be learned. Did you know that in one day approximately 9 percent of your time will be spent writing, 16 percent of your time will be spent reading, 30 percent of your time will be spent speaking, and 45 percent of your time will be spent listening?

We spend more time listening than any other activity, yet I've never seen a Christian training seminar that teaches you how to listen. It is possible to go to almost any graduation and see people getting awards for speaking, but I have never seen anyone get an award for listening. Remember the words of James: "So then, my beloved brethren, let every man be swift to hear, slow to speak, slow to wrath, for the wrath of man does not produce the righteousness of God" (1:19–20).

THE GOODNESS OF GOD

I would have lost heart, unless I had believed that I would see the goodness of the LORD in the land of the living.

PSALM 27:13

Idon't have to debate with you about the goodness of the Lord in the land of the living. We expect that as God's people, but sometimes we don't see it because we don't look for it. I've been keeping track of the goodness of God in the land of my living. I keep a little journal in which I write things God does. My list is growing. When I'm in trouble and my faith gets down to a flickering flame, I open up my journal and read my list, which shows the goodness of God in the land of my living. It has been a great encouragement to me.

God isn't on our time schedule. We need to remain calm when God delays. Sometimes when we pray, "Lord, help," He doesn't do it right away.

When trouble comes express, extend, experience, and enjoy your faith. When you pray in times of trouble, respond to God, rely on Him, resign to His will, and remain calm until His help arrives.

David Jeremiah

BE MY DISCIPLE

Take My yoke upon you and learn from Me, for I am gentle and lowly in heart, and you will find rest for your souls.

MATTHEW 11:29

There are two kinds of stress that people need to deal with. First is the stress of sin that is relieved when we come to Christ initially. But second is the stress that accumulates when we don't live our lives under Christ's lordship. That is the cause of the vast majority of the stress that Christians live with daily. To use Jesus' own words, it is the stress that comes from not taking Jesus' yoke upon us.

A yoke suggests a picture of oxen linked together pulling a common plow. That's not really what His words mean. Taking on a yoke was a rabbinical expression meaning to become a disciple of someone. Therefore, He is saying, "Come and be My disciple. Begin to let your life be patterned after the dictates of My life and My soul. Come and get involved in submission to Me in lordship. Take My yoke upon you."

Jesus, as the victorious Lord, the King of kings, is inviting us to be His disciples, to let Him rule over our lives.

PLUGGED IN

The LORD called Samuel. And he answered, "Here I am!"

I SAMUEL 3:4

Ernest Hemingway once lamented, "I live in a vacuum that is as lonely as a radio tube when the batteries are dead and there is no current to plug into."

Not so the Christian. We have a mission and a message. God has placed us on earth for a brief time to do an urgent work. Our lives have purpose, and all our days are scheduled in His perfect will. We travel an appointed way. What is the burning vision for your life? What does God want you to do?

Ask Him to show you. Read His Word, seeking His will for your life. Tell Him you're available. Say, like Samuel, "Here I am." Find something to do and begin doing it. Find a need and begin filling it.

Perhaps it's visiting someone in the hospital or nursing home or working with children in the church nursery. Perhaps it's singing in the choir, making visits for your church, or serving as an usher or greeter on Sunday morning.

Be faithful in that smaller things, and the Lord will give you more work to do, and more and more—all for His glory. He wants to use you. He has a purpose for your life, and He alone can give you a vision of His will.

David Jeremiah

THE SIN OF WORRY

Do not worry about your life, what you will eat; nor about the body, what you will put on. Life is more than food, and the body is more than clothing.

LUKE 12:22—23

Let me begin by stating something that you may or may not agree with: worry is sin. Worry is not part of our personality, it is not something to be excused because "everybody does it." From God's perspective, worry is sin. But in order to clarify this (it's important to know when we are sinning and when we are not), let's separate worry from concern.

It is certainly right to be concerned about things which are your responsibility and over which you exercise control. God expects us to be responsible, to be concerned that we follow through on what is ours to do. But worry is concerning yourself about things over which you have no control. Worry is allowing care and concern to escalate beyond the realm of responsibility and into a realm in which you have no authority or control—God's realm. And that kind of concern, which is worry, is sin.

When we worry, we deny the faithfulness of God—and that is why worry is sin.

LET IT BE

Mary, you are going to be with child in a way that no one has ever been with child before, or shall ever be afterward.

LUKE 1:35 (AUTHOR'S PARAPHRASE)

There are several ways humans come into being. Adam and Eve were created directly by God. They did not come through the birth process. Today, we are the products of a relationship between our mother and father. But Jesus was uniquely born in the sense that He was born of His mother, but He had no earthly father. So Mary was asked, at the age of sixteen, to comprehend a concept, a birth process, that had never before occurred in the history of humanity. No wonder she was perplexed!

This is the glory and wonder of Christmas, that God could plant not only into the womb of this woman the Son of God, but He could plant in her heart the faith to believe the message that she received from the angel. Her response has always overwhelmed me with a sense of absolute submission that ought to be in the heart of every child of God. Mary said, "Behold the maidservant of the Lord! Let it be to me according to your word."

David Jeremiah

CHILDREN ARE GIFTS
FROM GOD

Behold, children are a heritage from the LORD, the fruit of the womb is a reward.
PSALM 127:3

The Bible is clear in teaching us that our children are a gift from God. As far back as Genesis 4:1, we find Eve declaring that her son Cain had been given to her by God. Later, Abraham and Sarah had their son Isaac as a direct result of God's intervention in opening Sarah's womb. God also opened the womb of Leah, Jacob's first wife, and Rachel, also his wife. Ruth was also made a mother due to God's intervention (Ruth 4:13).

The little ones God gives to us do not come by accident or as interruptions to our lives. They come as God's good gifts to us, entrusted as a stewardship from Him. Children are not only given to receive love from their parents but to be God's teachers. What parent would say they have not learned about sacrifice, patience, priorities—not to mention learned more about God's love for us, His children—as a result of being a parent? Children are a gift for which parents should thank God every day.

DO NOT SEEK REVENGE

Repay no one evil for evil.

ROMANS 12:17

If you are seeking revenge, you have just opened your whole heart for Satan and his demons to take control of your life. Romans 12:17–21 teaches us what we are to do when we are tempted to revenge: "Repay no one evil for evil. Have regard for good things in the sight of all men. If it is possible, as much as depends on you, live peaceably with all men. Beloved, do not avenge yourselves, but rather give place to wrath; for it is written, 'Vengeance is mine, I will repay,' says the Lord. Therefore, if your enemy is hungry, feed him; if he is thirsty, give him a drink; for in so doing you will heap coals of fire on his head."

The Bible teaches that if we seek revenge, we are violating the principles of God and setting ourselves up for the control of Satan in our lives. When Jesus was under attack, He did not respond or seek to get even. He held Himself under control by the Spirit of God, and He serves as an example for all of us.

David Jeremiah

DON'T REJOICE IN SIN

[Love] does not rejoice in iniquity, but rejoices in the truth.

1 CORINTHIANS 13:6

In Greek, the phrase, "Love does not rejoice in iniquity," literally means, "Love does not take satisfaction from sin." To rejoice in unrighteousness is to justify sin. It is making wrong appear to be right. This is what Isaiah said in Isaiah 5:20: "Woe to those who call evil good, and good evil; who put darkness for light, and light for darkness."

There is much of that going on in our world today. Men and women in the media have come to understand that bad news is good news in the sense that it makes the headlines and provides more readership and listenership, but God's love is saddened when it hears of the defeats and tragedies in other people's lives. It is easy to be glad at another person's misfortune, but God says that as Christian people we are never to rejoice in sin. When you love somebody, you cover their sins; you don't broadcast them. John puts it this way: "I have no greater joy than to hear that my children walk in truth" (3 John v. 4).

THE GREATER MINISTRY

*This gospel of the kingdom will be preached in all the world as
a witness to all the nations.*

MATTHEW 24:14

I remember when television first came out. Many Christians
shunned it, believing it was run by the prince of the power
of the air. The evil one certainly had his influence in that
medium (and still does), but why not use television as a
means to proclaim the good news? Why not use radio? Why
not use print? Why not use the Internet? Why not use any
means at hand to take the message of the gospel and spread
it throughout the whole world? The farther the better. The
faster the better. The sooner the better. Until He comes!

What Jesus was saying to His disciples was this: "While
I was on this earth, I was localized, I could only touch individual men and women in My travels and speak to a few local
audiences. But believe Me, after I am gone and the Holy
Spirit comes to fill and empower My sons and daughters,
then My ministry will be as far spread as Christians are."

So wherever there is a Christian, there is Christ. Wherever
there is a believer, there is ministry.

David Jeremiah

A GOOD CONSCIENCE

*Then Paul, looking earnestly at the council, said, "Men and brethren,
I have lived in all good conscience before God until this day."*

ACTS 23:1

On August 18, 1788, as he prepared to become the first
president of the United States, George Washington
wrote to Alexander Hamilton, saying, "I hope I shall possess
firmness and virtue enough to maintain what I consider the
most enviable of all titles, the character of an honest man."

Character is to leadership what wood is to a tree—that
inner "stuff" that provides its sturdiness and strength. Many
a tree has blown down because it rotted on the inside. The
notion that a person's personal life has no bearing on his or
her leadership is an unbiblical streak of postmodern thinking that ravages not only leaders, but their followers as well.

Each of us is a leader—of a group, a home, a project, a
segment of God's work. We need to maintain a clear conscience and be worthy of the calling we've received. "I myself
always strive to have a conscience without offense toward
God and men," wrote Paul in Acts 24:16. That's important
not only for ourselves, but for those we're influencing.

GOD'S VIEW OF PROSPERITY

The keeper of the prison did not look into anything that was under Joseph's
authority, because the LORD was with him; and whatever he did,
the LORD made it prosper.

GENESIS 39:23

Think about Joseph's circumstances. He was a slave, bound to his master. Yet the Bible says he was prosperous. We have this idea in America that prosperity is related to money and possessions, but prosperity in the eyes of God refers to character. If we are true to the Lord and His Word, we are rich. If we are in His will, we have the assurance that all things work together for good, something we certainly see evident in the life of Joseph.

It has been said that God doesn't do anything or allow anything to be done to us that we would not choose for ourselves, if we could only see things from His perspective. If we could see every event exactly as God does, we would do things the very same way. He sees the end from the beginning, how everything fits together, and how necessary some of our hurts and disappointments are. Prosperity isn't a matter of circumstances, but a matter of character. When Scripture says that Joseph was prosperous, it has little to do with how many material possessions he had, but with how much of him God had. Even though a slave, Joseph was a prosperous man.

David Jeremiah

MASTER COMPANION

Fear not, for I have redeemed you; I have called you by your name; you are Mine.
ISAIAH 43:1

We need companionship. We need fellowship. God has built these needs into us. In those moments when we are between friends, in those dark caverns of being all alone, we have the Master Companion, who stays with us through it all.

> *Now, thus says the LORD, who created you, O Jacob.*
> *And He who formed you, O Israel:*
>
> *"Fear not, for I have redeemed you;*
> *I have called you by your name;*
> *You are Mine.*
> *When you pass through the waters, I will be with you;*
> *And through the rivers, they shall not overflow you.*
> *When you walk through the fire, you shall not be burned,*
> *Nor shall the flame scorch you.*
> *For I am the LORD your God,*
> *The Holy One of Israel, your Savior."* (Isaiah 43:1–3)

The prophet Isaiah reminds us that God's immediate presence in our lives is not affected by our circumstances.

THE GREATER MESSAGE

Do not rejoice in this, that the spirits are subject to you, but rather rejoice because your names are written in heaven.

LUKE 10:20

I read about a group of short-term missionaries who recently held evangelistic meetings in Africa. During those meetings, these believers reported, a blind man miraculously received his sight. When the believers came back to report to the sending churches, that was just about all they could talk about. Yet during those same meetings, many embraced Jesus Christ as Savior and found eternal salvation. Many stepped out of spiritual blindness into the light of God's kingdom. But that news always seemed to receive second billing to "the miracle." If we could only view these things as God does! The message of reconciliation meets the basic needs of every man and woman, every boy and girl. In miracles, only God's power and goodness are revealed, but in conversion, God's grace is revealed—something that causes even the angels to look over the rampart of heaven in wonder (1 Peter 1:12).

The message of the saving grace of God is the greater message. The death, burial, and resurrection of Jesus Christ have given to us in this generation the greatest message that has ever been communicated to any people. Anywhere. At any time. Period.

David Jeremiah

THE SOURCE OF SONG

He has put a new song in my mouth—praise to our God; many will see it and fear, and will trust in the LORD.

PSALM 40:3

Christianity is a religion of song. Agnosticism has no carols. Confucianism and Brahmanism have no anthems or alleluias. Dreary, weird dirges reveal no hope for the present or for the future. Christianity, however, is filled with music. Only the message of Christ puts a song in a person's heart.

When you have Christ in your heart, something changes inside of you, and a melody starts to form that you can't really control. It is unlike any other belief system.

As we read the stories of Christmas in the gospel of Luke, we find six different songs recorded almost back-to-back: the "Beatitude of Elizabeth," when she was visited by Mary; the "Magnificat of Mary," Mary's song; the "Benedictus of Zacharias," the father of John the Baptist; the "Song of Simeon," when he was presented with the Christ child at the temple; the "Evangel Song" of the angel of the Lord over the plains; and finally, the "Gloria" of the angelic hosts. When Jesus came into the world, music was reborn.

GO WITH HASTE

Now there were in the same country shepherds living out in the fields,
keeping watch over their flock by night.

LUKE 2:8

Christmas is the season of twinkling lights, shiny tinsel, and cheery holiday bells. Yet within the brightness of Christmas a dark paradox looms: Christmas is not the best but the worst time of year for many people. Suicides increase, loneliness is heightened, and broken families feel the pain of separation. People reason that the other eleven months of the year aren't necessarily supposed to be filled with joy—but Christmas is.

Loneliness, financial limitations, ill health . . . many things can quench the holiday spark. If you fear the feelings that come your way at Christmas, you're not alone. Another group of "forgotten" people heard a special message from the angels that first Christmas: "Fear not"! (Luke 2:10 KJV). The angels announced the One who would dispel all fear forever—Jesus Christ. The shepherds went "with haste" (v. 16). They didn't let fear stop them from meeting the Messiah.

Just as the shepherds cast aside their fears and immediately went to find Jesus, you can do the same this Christmas. Jesus is waiting to be found.

David Jeremiah

CELEBRATE HIS LOVE

Glory to God in the highest, and on earth peace, goodwill toward men!

LUKE 2:14

In more than a few past wars, the warring nations would call a cease-fire for Christmas Day. They would agree that on Christmas Day they wouldn't shoot at each other, drop bombs, or try to destroy one another. Then, of course, the day after Christmas they would start killing each other again.

As strange as that custom has been, in a wonderful way it is a mute testimony to the purpose for which Christ came—to bring peace. That was the message the angels proclaimed.

Today, there are many places in our world where *peace* is not a word in anyone's vocabulary. Yet every Christian knows that there is coming a time when peace will reign on this earth. Each Christmas season, a kind of new hope is born in our hearts—that though the outlook may be dark, we can look beyond today. The Prince of Peace has come and with Him the faith that someday men will beat their swords into plowshares and their spears into pruning hooks and we shall be at peace.

THE CRY OF LIFE

And she brought forth her firstborn Son.

LUKE 2:7

Life and especially history are full of all kinds of cries. There have been cries of anguish and joy, cries of victory and defeat. And yet there is probably no cry that is as touching, as tender, and as timely as the fragile first cry of a newborn babe.

If you are a parent, you know the delirious joy—indeed, relief—that came when your own babies shattered the delivery room air with their first cry. Why does a child's cry, something that normally brings concern to a parent, produce joy when it is first heard? Because it's a sign of *life*. The tension in the delivery room waiting on that first cry is not unlike the tension in all of creation that first Christmas Eve. When the cold silence of a Bethlehem night was broken by Jesus' first cry, it meant more than just life. It meant eternal life—spiritual life! No longer would mankind live in fear of death. Life itself had been born in Bethlehem.

History's most famous cry was that of a tiny Babe, born in a manger. Celebrate that cry of life this Christmas season. Even today, it echoes in your heart if you know Jesus Christ as a Savior.

David Jeremiah

Delight in the Lord

Delight yourself also in the Lord, and He shall give you the desires of your heart.
Psalm 37:4

Tracing the word *delight* through the Old Testament, I was surprised to learn that the majority of its uses are in relationship to the Word of God—delighting in the Word. The psalmists delighted in God's will as expressed in His law (Psalm 40:8); delighted in His statutes (119:16); delighted in His commandments (119:35); and delighted in His precepts and law (119:69–70, 77, 92, 174).

There is a profound relationship between delighting in the Lord and delighting in His Word. Think about your relationship with a person who is the object of your affections. Your conversations, the letters you receive, the phone calls you share—their words are a reflection of who they are. So to delight in that person's words is to delight in them. And the same is true of our relationship with God. To trust in God is also to delight in Him and His promises. No Christian who delights in what God says about the future ("I will provide for you") can also be found worrying about the future.

When delighting in the Lord is your focus, everything else is brought into perspective.

USE GOD'S STRENGTH

My grace is sufficient for you, for My strength is made perfect in weakness.
2 CORINTHIANS 12:9

When we try to live our lives in our own strength, we ultimately fail. And if we don't fail, we fall very short of God's purposes for us. When we operate in the flesh, three things are always true: (1) we will always lack the power of the Spirit, and we'll suffer from fatigue; (2) we will always lack the vision of the Spirit, so we'll suffer from frustration; and (3) we will always lack the sustaining ministry of the Spirit, so we'll suffer from failure.

Do these consequences sound familiar? You will always suffer these results when you tackle life in your own strength. But when tragedy strikes—an illness, financial hardship, rebellious children—you turn to God. When you feel helpless, inadequate, and weak, the Spirit of God gives you strength. All of a sudden you realize something dynamic is going on that you have never experienced before. It's not your power; it's God's power. The apostle Paul admits that if it takes weakness to get God's power in his life, he's better off weak than strong. Because when you are weak, then you are strong.

David Jeremiah

ENCOURAGEMENT IS URGENT

Let us encourage one another.

HEBREWS 10:25 NIV

I wear many hats as a parent, as all parents do. I am a provider, a leader, and a disciplinarian when necessary. But I believe my greatest responsibility is as a cheerleader. More than anything else, kids today need the supportive love, encouragement, and cheering-on of their parents. James Dobson, the family expert who spent years studying problems of adolescent behavior, once said in my presence, "Here's the distilled wisdom of all my research. Here is what you need to do if you have adolescents: just get them through it."

Just get them through it! Hang in there with them until the whitewater rapids of the teenage years are left behind.

Encouragement is an urgent need of our day. A church that does not equip its people as encouragers will soon phase out of any meaningful ministry in its community. God help us to learn how to be encouragers!

PROBLEMS PROMOTE MATURITY

Now no chastening seems to be joyful for the present, but painful; nevertheless, afterward it yields the peaceable fruit of righteousness to those who have been trained by it.

HEBREWS 12:11

The concept of gaining strength through difficulties is under assault today by those preaching success and prosperity. Some have claimed that, if we're Christians, God wants everything to be right and easy for us.

It certainly sounds spiritual to claim that those close to God ought never to experience failure or illness, but that has never been the message of the church. Rather than producing soldiers, that sort of thinking produces pampered children. There is no Bible verse, nor even an implied principle, that suggests our walk on earth should be free from trouble.

Problems are God's gifts to us to make us strong. And those who would keep us out of problems sometimes seek to short-circuit the plan of God. Problems are God's way of molding us into maturity, putting iron into our souls so that we can face the challenges ahead. Problems promote maturity.

David Jeremiah

EVER-PRESENT GOD

God is . . . a very present help in trouble.

PSALM 46:1

"God is . . . a very present help in trouble." God is not just present; He is very present! It's like you telling a good friend that you are available to help them if they need you. "Oh, I hate to bother you," they reply. "No," you counter, "I am very much available for you. Just let me know when." You are saying, "I am ever-available." And that's how God is for us. He is the most accessible help we could ever imagine.

The word for *trouble* could be rendered as a "tight place." God is ever-present to help us in the tight places we get into in life, when we are between a rock and a hard place. If someone is ever-present, it means they are easy to be found. We don't have to go looking for them. In fact, we can't. We're stuck in a tight place!

The reason God is always with us, even in our tight places, is because of what He told Moses in Exodus 33:14:"My presence will go with you." So when we are stuck and can't move, God is there because He is always with us.

FELLOWSHIP FOREVER

Behold, the tabernacle of God is with men, and He will dwell with them, and they shall be His people. God Himself will be with them and be their God.

REVELATION 21:3

There will be no sanctuary or tabernacle or temple in heaven—and no churches. Revelation 21:22 says that "the Lord God Almighty and the Lamb are its temple." Because God will be dwelling in the midst of His people, just as He started off doing in the garden of Eden, there will be no need for a sanctuary for Him to dwell in.

We incorrectly call our churches "sanctuaries" today because they are where we draw together once a week to worship God and hear His Word proclaimed. But God does not dwell in buildings in this age; He dwells in His people. At present, we cannot "see" His presence as we will be able to in heaven. Instead of dwelling "in" us in heaven, He will dwell "among" us, in our very presence.

The same Jesus who healed the sick, raised the dead, fed the multitudes, died on Calvary, was raised from the dead, and ascended into heaven will be walking among us in heaven. We will have unbroken, personal fellowship with Him forever.

David Jeremiah

SOURCES

Exposing the Myths of Parenthood. Jeremiah, David, with Carole C.
    Carson. Dallas: Word Publishing, 1988.

A Nation in Crisis, vol. 1. Atlanta: Walk thru the Bible, 1996.

Book of Esther, The. Atlanta: Walk thru the Bible, 1994.

Celebrate His Love. Atlanta: Walk thru the Bible, 1999.

Christ's Death and Resurrection. Atlanta: Walk thru the Bible, 1997.

Christians Have Stress Too. San Diego: Turning Point, 2000.

Escape the Coming Night study guide, vol. 4. San Diego: Turning
    Point, 2000.

Facing the Giants in Your Life. San Diego: Turning Point, 2001.

Fruit of the Spirit. Atlanta: Walk thru the Bible, 1995.

Gifts from God study guide. San Diego: Turning Point, 1999.

Giving to God. San Diego: Turning Point, 2001.

God in You. Sisters, OR: Multnomah, 1998.

God Meant It for Good: The Life of Joseph, vol. 1. San Diego: Turning
    Point, 1996.

God Meant It for Good: The Life of Joseph, vol. 2. San Diego: Turning
    Point, 1996.

God's Righteousness and Man's Rebellion. Living by Faith series, vol.
    4. San Diego: Turning Point, 2002.

God's Sovereignty and Man's Responsibility. Living by Faith series, vol.
    4. San Diego: Turning Point, 2002.

Greatest Stories Ever Told, The. Atlanta: Walk thru the Bible, 2000.

Hearing the Master's Voice. San Diego: Turning Point, 1999.

Heroes of the Faith. San Diego: Turning Point, 2001.

Home and Family. San Diego: Turning Point, 2000.

Home Improvement. San Diego: Turning Point, 2001.

How to Be Happy According to Jesus. Atlanta: Walk thru the Bible, 1996.

In Transit: Moving Confidently through Today's World. Wheaton, IL: Tyndale, 1984.

Investing for Eternity. Atlanta: Walk Thru the Bible, 1999.

Jesus' Final Warning study guide. Atlanta: Walk thru the Bible, 1999.

Knowing the God You Worship. Atlanta: Walk thru the Bible, 1994.

Love in Action. San Diego: Turning Point, 2001.

Man's Ruin and Christ's Redemption. Living by Faith series, vol. 2. San Diego: Turning Point, 2000.

My Heart's Desire: Living Every Moment in the Wonder of Worship. Brentwood, TN: Integrity, 2002.

Overcoming Loneliness study guide. Atlanta: Walk thru the Bible, 1997.

Overcoming Loneliness. Nashville: Thomas Nelson, 1991.

People God Uses, The. San Diego: Turning Point, 2000.

People Who Met Jesus. San Diego: Turning Point, 2000.

Power of Encouragement, The. Sisters, OR: Multnomah, 1997

Power of Love, The. Atlanta: Walk thru the Bible, 1994.

Powerful Principles from Proverbs. San Diego: Turning Point, 2002.

Prayer—The Great Adventure study guide. San Diego: Turning Point, 2000.

Prophetic Turning Points. San Diego: Turning Point, 2001.

Runaway Prophet—Jonah, The. San Diego: Turning Point, 1998.

Ruth, Romance, and Redemption. San Diego: Turning Point, 1999.

Signs of the Second Coming. Atlanta: Walk thru the Bible, 1996.

Sons of God and the Spirit of God, The. Living by Faith series, vol. 3. San Diego: Turning Point, 2000.

Spiritual Warfare. San Diego: Turning Point, 2002.

Ten Burning Questions from Psalms. San Diego: Turning Point, 1994.

Turning Points magazine and devotional guide, vol. 3, no. 7 (December 2001). vol. 4, no. 2 (March 2002); vol. 4, no. 3 (April 2002); vol. 4, no. 4 (May 2002); vol. 4, no. 5 (June

2002); vol. 4, no. 6 (July 2002); vol. 4, no. 7 (August 2002).

Turning Toward Joy. Colorado Springs: Chariot Victor, 1992.

Turning Toward Integrity study guide. Atlanta: Walk thru the Bible, 2000.

What the Bible Says about Angels study guide. San Diego: Turning Point, 1999.

Worship. Atlanta: Walk thru the Bible, 1995.

NOTES

NOTES

NOTES

NOTES

NOTES

NOTES